THE PENDULUM OF WAR
THE FIGHT FOR UPPER CANADA,
JANUARY–JUNE 1813

UPPER CANADA PRESERVED
WAR OF 1812

THE PENDULUM OF WAR

THE FIGHT FOR UPPER CANADA, JANUARY–JUNE 1813

RICHARD FELTOE

DUNDURN
TORONTO

Editor: Cheryl Hawley
Design: Jennifer Scott
Printer: Webcom

Library and Archives Canada Cataloguing in Publication

Feltoe, Richard, 1954-
The pendulum of war : the fight for Upper Canada, January-June 1813 / by Richard Feltoe.

(Upper Canada preserved, War of 1812)
Includes bibliographical references and index.
Issued also in electronic formats.
ISBN 978-1-4597-0699-6

1. Canada--History--War of 1812--Campaigns. 2. Canada--History--War of 1812--Battlefields. 3. Canada--History--War of 1812--Personal narratives. I. Title. II. Series: Feltoe, Richard, 1954- Upper Canada preserved, War of 1812.

FC442.F439 2013   971.03'4   C2012-904599-3

1   2   3   4   5   17   16   15   14   13

Conseil des Arts du Canada Canada Council for the Arts   Canada   ONTARIO ARTS COUNCIL / CONSEIL DES ARTS DE L'ONTARIO

We acknowledge the support of the **Canada Council for the Arts** and the **Ontario Arts Council** for our publishing program. We also acknowledge the financial support of the **Government of Canada** through the **Canada Book Fund** and **Livres Canada Books**, and the **Government of Ontario** through the **Ontario Book Publishing Tax Credit** and the **Ontario Media Development Corporation**.

Printed and bound in Canada.

Unless otherwise attributed, images and maps are the property and copyright of the author.

Visit us at
Dundurn.com | Definingcanada.ca | @dundurnpress | Facebook.com/dundurnpress

Dundurn
3 Church Street, Suite 500
Toronto, Ontario, Canada
M5E 1M2

Gazelle Book Services Limited
White Cross Mills
High Town, Lancaster, England
LA1 4XS

Dundurn
2250 Military Road
Tonawanda, NY
U.S.A. 14150

This book is offered:

First, as a salute to the memory of all those, on both sides of the lines, who served, sacrificed, and died as they loyally obeyed their country's call-to-arms in the North American War of 1812–1815.

Second, as a mark of respect to the men and women of the military services of Canada, Great Britain, and the United States, who today honorably continue that legacy of service and sacrifice at home and across the globe.

Third, as a thank-you to my fellow "Living History" reenactors, with and against whom I've "fought" for so many years.

Finally, as a legacy for my grandsons, Anthony, Lawrence, and Daniel.

TABLE OF CONTENTS

ACKNOWLEDGEMENTS

As I detailed in the first part of this series, no publication is realistically the work of a single individual, or the author in isolation, and this series is no exception. As such, I can only hope to assure all those who have given their support and encouragement that their efforts are deeply and gratefully appreciated by me, but page space forbids their individual mention. Therefore, I must restrict myself to naming and thanking but a few, whilst saluting the many.

To my wife, Diane, my social, book signings, and speaking appointments coordinator, marketing manager, chief accountant, and communications secretary. Thanks for putting up with all of this … Two down and only four to go! Until the next ones…

To my friend and fellow historian Pat Kavanagh…Once again, your generosity in providing me unrestricted access to your vast resource collection of American records, official documents, and personal letters on the war has brought forward a treasure trove of historical information. Without your aid and resources, this work could not have been created. I thank you, sir.

To my fellow author and staunch Canadian nationalist, Donald Graves… Your example of meticulous and comprehensive research, as well as your efforts to have the service and sacrifice of the Canadian regiments involved in the War of 1812 recognized, is a lesson and example that I can only hope to emulate in my modest works.

To the many dedicated staff members of the numerous museums, archives, and libraries that I visited to undertake the research for this work and who cheerfully assisted my searches to fruition…

Your dedication and expertise is a National treasure that cannot be measured or underestimated.

Penultimately, I cannot fail to acknowledge the guidance and support provided by my editor Cheryl Hawley, my designer Jennifer Scott, as well as the whole creative team at Dundurn Press in turning this idea into a reality.

Finally, to Karen, my friend and guide, whose combination of fierce editorial and literary criticism, backed by an equally dedicated and unequivocal support of the value of my writings, helped to create the work that is now evolving in these pages… You may not have lived to see this work completed, but your spirit and love of our history and heritage lives on within it.

Thank You!
Richard Feltoe

PREFACE

VARIATIONS

As more fully outlined in the introduction to the first part of this series, the historic material included here includes variations in spelling, jargon, and place name changes that have occurred over time. As a result, the following standards have been applied.

- Where variations on spelling in quotes are found, the material has been repeatedly checked to ensure its accuracy and is presented just as it was found in the original documents and without the term [*sic*].
- While generally recognized military terms are presented as is, some of the more archaic or jargon-type words are either followed by a modern equivalent word or referenced in a separate glossary of terms. In a similar manner, maintaining the differential identification of military units from the two principal combatant nations, (when both used a system of numbers to designate their regiments) has been achieved by showing British Regimental numbers as numerals (41st Regiment, 89th Regiment, etc.) and where required with their subsidiary titles (1st (Royal Scots) Regiment, 8th (King's) Regiment), whilst the American Regiments are expressed as words (First Regiment, Twenty-Fifth Regiment, etc.).
- Where place names appear with a number of variants (e.g., Sackett's Harbour, Sacket's Harbour, Sakets Harbor, or Sacket's Harbor) I have adopted a single format for each case, based upon a judgment of what I felt was the

predominant version used at the time. Where names have changed entirely, or would cause needless confusion (Newark becoming Niagara and currently Niagara-on-the-Lake), I have generally gone with what would clarify the location and simplify identification overall or included a reference to the modern name (Crossroads becoming Virgil).

Finally, in including images where there is both a period and modern image combined for a then-and-now effect, I have tried, as far as possible, to obtain the same relative perspective — subject to the limitations imposed where the physical landscape and property ownership make it possible to do so.

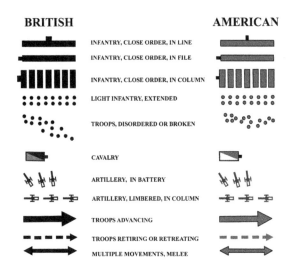

CHAPTER 1

Introduction

On June 18, 1812, United States President James Madison signed a declaration of war against Great Britain. Ostensibly, this war was to redress America's long-standing grievances over Atlantic maritime trading rights and offences against U.S. citizens being "press ganged" into the Royal Navy. However, it also had the underlying goal of eliminating the presence and influence of Great Britain on the North American continent — a situation promoted by a group of militant U.S. nationalists ("War Hawks"), pressing an expansionist cause that in later decades would be referred to as manifest destiny. Publicly, this war was promoted as simply requiring U.S. troops to march into the welcoming heart of Britain's Canadian colonies and evict the veteran colonial power without significant difficulty or complications before the end of the year. However, once it began, the reality of the war in 1812 to conquer Canada turned out to be something else entirely, and a nasty surprise to boot — one where the Americans lost every major engagement in which they fought.

This earlier part of the story is recounted in the first book in this six-part series, *The Call to Arms*. This work, *The Pendulum of War*, takes up that story in order to trace the course of the war into the first six months of 1813 on the "Northern" frontier. For those who have not read the first work, the following timeline should provide a background to the events that are documented here.

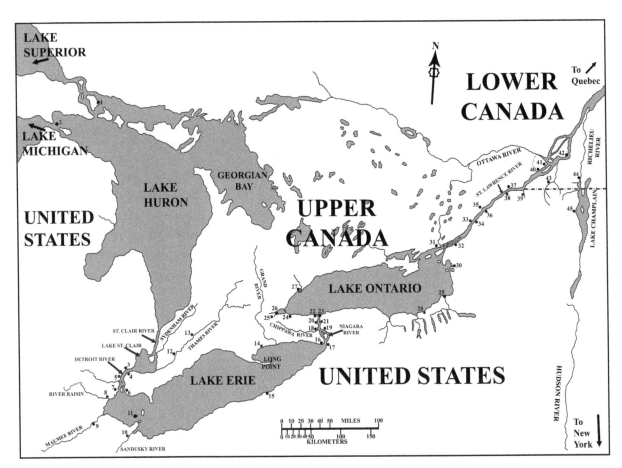

The "Northern Frontier" of the War of 1812–1815

THE "NORTHERN FRONTIER" OF THE WAR OF 1812–1815

(Modern Name)   [Fortifications]

1. St. Joseph Island [Fort St. Joseph]
2. Michilimackinac Island (Mackinac) [Fort Mackinac/Fort Michilimackinac]
3. Detroit [Fort Detroit]
4. Sandwich (Windsor)
5. Monguagon/Maguaga
6. Amherstburg (Malden) [Fort Amherstburg]
7. Brownstown
8. Frenchtown
9. Perrysburg [Fort Meigs]
10. [Fort Stephenson]
11. Put-in-Bay
12. Moravianstown
13. Longwoods
14. Port Dover
15. Presque Isle (Erie, PA)
16. Fort Erie [Fort Erie]
17. Buffalo and Black Rock
18. Chippawa
19. [Fort Schlosser]
20. Queenston
21. Lewiston
22. Newark (Niagara-on-the-Lake) [Fort George, Fort Mississauga]
23. [Fort Niagara]
24. Stoney Creek
25. Ancaster
26. Burlington Heights (Hamilton)
27. York (Toronto) [Fort York]
28. Sodus
29. Oswego [Fort Oswego]
30. Sackets Harbor [Fort Tompkins, Fort Volunteer, Fort Pike]
31. Kingston [Fort Frederick, Fort Henry]
32. French Creek
33. Elizabethtown/Brockville (1813)
34. Morrisburg
35. Prescott [Fort Wellington]
36. Ogdensburg
37. Crysler's Farm
38. Hamilton (Waddington, NY)
39. French Mills
40. Coteau-du-Lac
41. Cedars
42. Montreal
43. Châteauguay
44. Isle-aux-Noix
45. Plattsburg

TIMELINE OF EVENTS

- November 4, 1811: [Washington] In U.S. congressional elections, anti-British War Hawk representatives dominate the new electoral body of Congress.

- December 6, 1811: [Washington] U.S. War Hawk Peter B. Porter, chairman of the Foreign Relations Committee, reports to the Senate, advocating his committee's position of declaring war against Great Britain by way of invading and occupying its Canadian colonies.

- June 17/18, 1812: [Washington] The U.S. Senate passes the vote to declare war on Great Britain. President Madison signs the declaration of war.

- July 1–2, 1812: [Detroit frontier] News of the U.S. declaration of war reaches Fort Amherstburg (Malden) at Amherstburg (Upper Canada) before it is received by the U.S. forces on the other side of the Detroit River. This allows British forces to surprise, intercept, and capture the U.S. vessel *Cuyahoga*, finding on board the entire military papers of Brigadier General William Hull and revealing vital intelligence of U.S. plans and dispositions for the Detroit frontier.

- July 12, 1812: [Detroit frontier] Despite the loss of his papers, Brigadier General Hull launches an invasion of Upper Canada at Sandwich

(Windsor). Hull then issues a proclamation of "liberation" to the residents of Upper Canada.

- July 15–17, 1812: [Upper Canada] News of the declaration of war reaches the British Fort St. Joseph, at the head of Lake Huron, before the nearby American base at Michilimackinac (Mackinac). In response, a combined force of British, Canadian, and Native troops mount an attack against the unprepared American garrison, forcing it to surrender without a shot being fired.

- July 22, 1812: [Upper Canada] Upper Canada governor, Major General Isaac Brock, issues an official rebuttal and repudiation of General Hull's demands for the surrender of Upper Canada to the Americans.

- August 1, 1812: [Lower Canada] News arrives at Quebec City that the British government has repealed its contentious Orders-in-Council affecting American maritime trading rights with Britain's wartime enemy, France. Because these issues were cited by the American government as the principal reason and cause for the war being declared, Sir George Provost writes to Major General Henry Dearborn, recommending an armistice until the U.S. government's position on settling the outstanding issues between the two governments is known. As a result, a regional suspension of hostilities is established.

- August 11, 1812: [Detroit frontier] Hearing that Major General Brock is sending reinforcements to the Detroit frontier, Brigadier General Hull abandons the American invasion into Upper Canada and retreats back across the Detroit River

- August 13, 1812: [Washington] President Madison and Secretary of War William Eustis officially reject the armistice proposals made by Sir George Prevost and order a recommencement of hostilities to conquer Canada.

- August 16, 1812: [Detroit frontier] British forces under Major General Brock, supported by Native allies under Tecumseh, cross the Detroit River, advance on Detroit, and intimidate Brigadier General Hull into surrendering his entire garrison. In addition, the Territory of Michigan is deemed as being ceded to the British Crown and becomes a de-facto part of Upper Canada.

- October 13, 1812: [Niagara frontier] The Battle of Queenston Heights. U.S. forces invade Upper Canada at Queenston and succeed in establishing a beachhead that controls the village and the "heights." Major General Brock is killed leading a direct frontal counterattack. Later in the day, Major General Roger Sheaffe arrives with reinforcements from Fort George at Newark, leads a successful flanking counterattack upon the American position, and routs their line. During the course of the battle, many U.S. militia troops stand on their constitutional rights and refuse to cross into Upper Canada to participate in the invasion.

- November 28, 1812: [Niagara frontier] The Battle of Frenchman's Creek. U.S. forces make landings at Fort Erie and Frenchman's Creek in an attempt to create a bridgehead for an invasion. While initially successful and overrunning the riverside batteries, British countermoves cause many American troops to abandon the attempt and leave in the remaining boats, stranding the remainder of the American force. As a result, British counterattacks quickly retake the positions and fend off a follow-up wave of American boats bringing reinforcements. In response, U.S. forces at Buffalo effectively mutiny against their commander, Brigadier General Alexander Smyth, and the threat of invasion of Upper Canada collapses on the Niagara frontier.

- December 3, 1812: [Washington] U.S. Secretary of War William Eustis resigns under a cloud of criticism for his mishandling of the American war effort to date.

CHAPTER 2

Pre-emptive Strikes

As 1813 began, the military events of 1812 played a major role in the plans developed by both sides for the upcoming campaign season. To the American government, its previous military defeats were embarrassments, but ones that could be rectified by the provision of future victories. On the other hand, the loss of the Territory of Michigan to the authority of the British Crown as part of the surrender at Detroit was a political disaster that almost toppled the administration and was looked on as a stain upon the national pride of the United States.

Furthermore, following Hull's surrender, reports accumulated of Native warriors from the British alliance robbing and attacking wounded or sick American soldiers, terrorizing civilians, and looting isolated homes. Although these reports also repeatedly documented that whenever they were around, the British troops and their officers tried to restrain or prevent these depredations, these details of fact were not allowed to mitigate the political advantage these events gave to the War Hawks in calling for a massive retaliatory expansion of the American war effort.

One particularly vehement congressman, Henry Clay, stated:

> Canada innocent? Canada unoffending? Is it not in Canada that the tomahawk of the savage has been moulded into its death-like form? Has it not been from Canadian magazines, Malden [Amherstburg] and others, that these supplies have been issued? Supplies which have

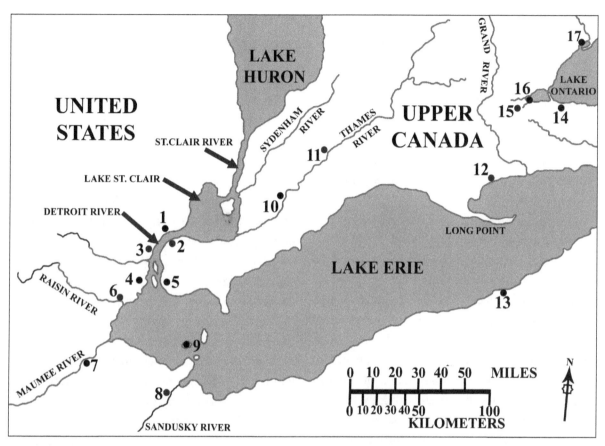

THE DETROIT FRONTIER

1. Detroit [Fort Detroit]
2. Sandwich (Windsor)
3. Monguagon/Maguaga
4. Brownstown
5. Amherstburg [Fort Amherstburg/Fort Malden]
6. Frenchtown
7. Perrysburg [Fort Meigs]
8. [Fort Stephenson]

9. Put-in-Bay
10. Moravianstown
11. Longwoods
12. Port Dover
13. Presque Isle (Erie, PA)
14. Stoney Creek
15. Ancaster
16. Burlington Heights
17. York (Toronto) [Fort York]

enabled the savage hordes to butcher the garrison of Chicago and to commit other horrid murders? Was it not by the joint co-operation of Canadians and Indians that a remote American fort Michilimackinac, was assailed and reduced while in ignorance of war? What does this war represent? The united energies of one people arrayed against the combined energies of another![1]

North of the border, Sir George Prevost, the senior British commander, also saw this ceding as a worst-case scenario. Only from his point of view, his troops' occupation of Michigan would become a cause that would unite the chronically divided political cabals in Washington, and precipitate a major backlash of American public opinion in favour of the continuation of the war. Despite his personal desire to withdraw his military forces back across the Detroit River and hand the territory back to American control, the need to maintain the vital Native support in preserving Upper Canada effectively forced Prevost to maintain the occupation. On the other hand, he was just as determined not to send any of his extensive reserves of troops or supplies west into Upper Canada, or beyond, to bolster the British positions; instead, his principal focus of protecting and maintaining Lower Canada and the Maritime colonies remained paramount.

At the same time, Prevost's local commander, Colonel Henry Proctor, was in a no-win situation. Isolated at the far end of a tenuous and intermittent supply line with a miniscule force of worn-out regular troops and a militia of varying degrees of enthusiasm and loyalty, Proctor was expected to not only defend his frontier in Upper Canada, but also occupy, control, and defend a huge new undefined border against the threat of American military retaliation. He was also responsible for maintaining an alliance with an unreliable and constantly changing balance of power within the Native nations, who demanded he uphold their claims on the newly occupied territory; not to mention supply their warriors and dependents with their every need in food and supplies. At the same time, he had inherited a huge region of American territory, occupied by potentially or actively hostile civilian settlers who demanded his protection against the hostilities of his Native allies. Finally, he had reliable intelligence that the U.S. military were indeed preparing a large expeditionary force to retake Michigan, Detroit, and press on into Upper Canada.

As a result, he recognized that if he maintained his extended positions, he could not possibly hold out against an American counter assault. On the other hand, if he retreated it would mean abandoning Michigan's civilian populace to probable escalating Native violence; while at the same time alienating those same Natives as being an abandonment of his treaty obligations. This, in turn, would threaten their further support of the British war effort and make them more likely to commit the very atrocities he was desperate to prevent in the first place.

THE BATTLE OF THE RIVER RAISIN (FRENCHTOWN), JANUARY 22, 1813

Matters came to a head in early January 1813, when a force of over 6,300 American troops of the "Northwestern Army" under Indiana Governor Major General William H. Harrison began their campaign to retake the Michigan Territory and Detroit. With this task completed, they were then to cross the ice on the Detroit River and capture Amherstburg before marching up the Thames River Valley to attack Burlington Heights and the Niagara frontier from the rear (west). Facing this force, Proctor's official roster of regular troops for the whole frontier consisted of some 12 officers and 367 other ranks, of which 114 were detached as the garrison at Detroit. His available militia forces were an unknown factor, as it would depend on how many actually responded to a call to arms. Finally,

his Native allies were proving to be less and less co-operative, as many warriors had angrily abandoned the frontier in response to hearing of Sir George Prevost's temporary armistice with the Americans at the end of the previous year.

Because of the huge logistical difficulties of engaging in a winter campaign, the American force advanced in three separate columns. Unfortunately, due to weather and transportation difficulties, inter-column communications soon broke down and the individual units in each column became strung out along their line-of-march. As a result, the isolated advance elements of the column under Brigadier General James Winchester reached the Maumee River Rapids on January 10th, well ahead of the remainder of their force. Despite having little in the way of proper winter clothing, suffering from malnutrition, disease, frostbite, and poor morale, the 1,300 men of the column still posed a significant threat to Proctor's small detachment of militia and Natives stationed at Frenchtown (Monroe, MI), some thirty-five miles (56 kilometers) away. Eighteen miles (29 kilometers) further on, at Amherstburg, Proctor was notified of this American threat and issued orders for his troops to prepare for action.

At Brigadier General Winchester's headquarters, confident that Major General Harrison was forwarding reinforcements to his position, Winchester authorized the seizure of Frenchtown by a detachment of 500 Kentucky militia. Augmented on the march to around 700 men, the Americans made their attack in three separate columns over the frozen River Raisin late in the afternoon of January 18th. Awaiting them were an alerted detachment of two small companies of Essex County Militia under the command of Major Ebenezer Reynolds, totalling only around fifty men, but supported by a small artillery howitzer and between 200 to 300 Native warriors.[2]

After an initial exchange of fire, the Americans advanced and outflanked the British position, forcing the defenders to make a fighting retreat into the woods, inflicting an estimated loss of twelve killed and fifty-five wounded on the Americans, for a loss on the defender's part of fifteen warriors killed, one militiaman wounded, and two militiamen and a warrior captured.[3] Having gained a victory, the American force occupied the village and were soon reinforced by the arrival of General Winchester with a further 250 regular troops. However, in occupying Frenchtown, Winchester made little subsequent effort to make the position more secure from a potential enemy attack — a failure that was to cost him and his men dearly in the days to come.

Informed of the American attack at 2:00 a.m. on January 19th, Colonel Proctor was concerned that additional American forces were moving to support Winchester's advance. He therefore moved quickly, trusting in the advantage of the moment to hit back at the enemy while their forces were divided. Leaving Amherstburg at dawn on January 20th, before all of the available militia units had arrived, his combined force of around 1,200 men made a forced march undetected by the enemy and were in striking range by the night of the 21st.

Before dawn on the 22nd, Proctor's troops were in position only a matter of two hundred yards (183 meters) from the unprepared American camp and began their final approach. Inside the camp, the normal daily morning call to reveille was almost immediately followed by the sounds of muskets being fired by the American sentries, who saw their enemy forming up for the attack. However, instead of advancing immediately with his entire force against a surprised and unprepared enemy, Proctor ordered his artillery to open fire in reply and held back the infantry. As a result, the otherwise shocked American troops were given time to react and form up. However, not having prepared any defences, the Americans were forced to fight where they stood. During the next hour, the battle fluctuated across the frozen fields and among the buildings of Frenchtown, with the American artillery and Kentucky militias at the American centre inflicting heavy casualties within the centre of the British line.

On the flanks the scene was even more chaotic, as the British Native allies and militias pressed home their attacks until they eventually broke through to the American rear. At that point the American flank positions began to crumble, with men scrambling to cross the frozen River Raisin. What followed was a rout that saw the Native warriors take full advantage of the heat of battle to exact revenge on the fleeing American troops, particularly men of the Kentucky militias. As a result, nearly four hundred were killed and an unrecorded number were listed as missing. Some American newspaper accounts even went so far as to claim that of a thousand men involved, only thirty-three evaded death or capture to return to their homes.

Among the prisoners captured was Brigadier General James Winchester, who was subsequently handed over to Colonel Proctor. Following a number of acrimonious exchanges about the respective excesses of the Native and Kentucky forces, Proctor and Winchester finally hammered out an agreement of surrender for those troops still holding out in a fortified blockhouse. Despite having achieved a stunning victory, over five hundred American prisoners then had to be fed, guarded, and protected from further Native attacks by Proctor's limited number of non-Native troops, which itself had been reduced through battle casualties by over two hundred men.

Following the battle, prisoner's claims that Major General Harrison and his column were only a matter of hours away persuaded Proctor that he had no realistic option but to retreat to Amherstburg with his able-bodied prisoners. However, without sufficient sleighs to carry both the British and American wounded, and believing Harrison's forces would be there within a matter of hours to tend to them, Proctor made the fateful decision to leave around sixty American wounded in the hospital and buildings at Frenchtown.

What was not known at the time was that Harrison's army was still more than forty miles away, nearly two days march. Shortly after noon on January 22nd, the British evacuated Frenchtown with their prisoners, arriving at Amherstburg shortly after midnight. There they were greeted by a jubilant crowd that applauded the victors, but who also had to be restrained from assaulting the Kentucky militia prisoners, who had been responsible for extensive looting and atrocities during the initial invasion of Upper Canada the previous summer. So violent were the feelings against these men that Prevost felt that although officially they could be paroled, their unarmed release on the Detroit frontier could imperil their lives at the hands of both the local citizenry and Native warriors alike. He therefore ordered their being marched, along with the captured regulars and

General Winchester, to the Niagara frontier for parole and subsequent release; while the general and the regulars continued on to the prison hulks at Quebec.

Meanwhile, hearing of Winchester's defeat, Harrison abandoned his advance and ordered a retreat back to the Maumee Rapids. After destroying Winchester's stockpile of supplies and making no attempt to determine the enemy's location or intentions, he continued his retreat to the Sandusky River, leaving the wounded Americans at Frenchtown abandoned and defenceless when, on the morning of January 23, 1813, a force of over two hundred Native warriors, unencumbered by any British or white restraints, descended on the village. They then began to rob the wounded Americans of their clothing, tomahawked any who were unable to move, herded the walking wounded out into the freezing air in little more than their shirtsleeves, and set fire to the buildings. What followed was a "death march" as around four or five dozen hapless prisoners were marched off into captivity, with any who faltered being summarily executed.

Hearing of this atrocity, Colonel Proctor and his subordinates made strenuous efforts to locate and ransom these prisoners. However, the political damage had been done. Even when American survivors subsequently testified that there had been no involvement, collusion, or even presence of British troops at the event, the fact that Colonel Proctor was subsequently promoted to the rank of Brigadier General, coupled with fictitious accounts and vitriolic cartoons showing smiling British troops and their officers standing by as the massacre occurred, filled the pages of American papers for months to come. The event even became a rallying cry, as "Remember the Raisin" entered the American lexicon of famous sayings related to the War of 1812.

Once again an American invasion had been thwarted, although at a long-term cost of raising the level of American determination to recover their lost territories and continue the war. In the short-term, however, it had the effect of making the American administration, and its new appointee to the position of secretary of war, Major General John Armstrong, wary of conducting operations at such a remote distance from its centre of supplies and logistics. Instead, Armstrong looked at pursuing the main American spring campaign at points along the St. Lawrence River, Lake Ontario, and on the Niagara frontier. Unfortunately for the American plans, the British forces on the St. Lawrence corridor had other ideas on that score.

THE RAID ON OGDENSBURG, FEBRUARY 22, 1813

From the outset of the war, the fact that the St. Lawrence River was being the single line of transport into Upper Canada had been a significant weakness in the British war effort. However, despite this obvious fact, the Americans made little real effort to dominate the waterway when war was first declared. In fact, apart from some initial skirmishes between gunboats, the only real cross-border incident came when the Americans made a sortie on Gananoque, just to the east of Kingston, on September 21, 1812.

However, the potential threat level rose in early October, when a force of the First Rifle Regiment under Captain Benjamin Forsyth and several companies of New York State militia under Brigadier General Jacob Brown were sent from Sackets Harbor to garrison the small community of Ogdensburg, directly opposite the British fortifications at Prescott. Up to this point, the civilian populace of Ogdensburg had maintained a friendly and highly profitable neutrality with their "enemy" by supplying cattle and other food to the Prescott garrison. This communication was now halted and British boats were fired on as they plied the water of the river.

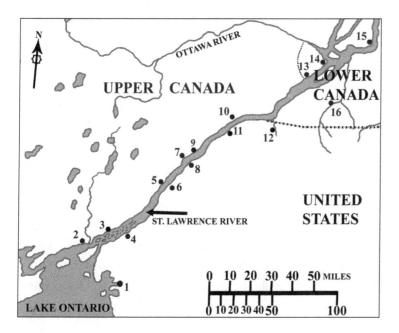

THE ST. LAWRENCE FRONTIER

1. Sackets Harbor
2. Kingston
3. Gananoque
4. French Creek
5. Elizabethtown/Brockville (1813)
6. Morrisburg (Morrisville)
7. Prescott
8. Ogdensburg
9. Matilda (Iroquois)
10. Crysler's Farm
11. Hamilton (Waddington, NY)
12. French Mills
13. Coteau-du-Lac
14. Cedars
15. Montreal
16. Châteauguay

In retaliation, the garrison at Prescott, under Colonel Robert Lethbridge, attempted to mount an attack against Ogdensburg on Sunday, October 4, 1812. Because Lethbridge made no effort to disguise his preparations, the British intentions were clearly telegraphed to the Americans, allowing the Ogdensburg garrison of around 1,200 men to be fully prepared when the attack commenced. As the British boats approached the enemy shore, they came under heavy American artillery and musket

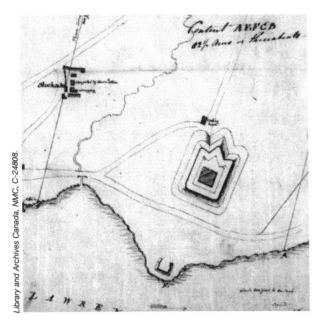

Detail from a map showing the fortifications at Prescott. What was later named Fort Wellington is at centre right, while a small stockaded military compound lies just to the left (west).

fire, which inflicted significant damage on the vessels and casualties amongst the tightly packed men. Unable to sustain the attack, the assault collapsed, to the humiliation of the British and the added prestige of the American military commanders. In response, Colonel Lethbridge was replaced by a far more experienced combat officer, Lieutenant Colonel Thomas Pearson (23rd Regiment), who undertook to bring the garrison at Prescott up to a proper state of battle readiness and made detailed plans for the destruction of Ogdensburg. Unfortunately, Prevost's non-aggression directives vetoed any immediate retaliation.

With the New Year little seemed to have changed, as the uneasy stalemate of truce continued. However, at the beginning of February Captain Forsyth received reports that a number of American troops were being held and mistreated in the jail at Elizabethtown (Brockville). Without verifying the information, and against general orders, Forsyth organized a raiding party consisting of around two hundred U.S. riflemen, supported by Ogdensburg militiamen under Colonel Thomas Benedict. Crossing the frozen St. Lawrence River undetected on the night of February 6–7th, the Americans swept down on the detachment of Leeds County Militia garrisoning the post, capturing them almost without a shot being fired. Releasing the few prisoners that they found in the jail cells, the Americans then arrested a number of local citizens to add to the twenty or so militiamen already captured and returned to the Ogdensburg with over fifty prisoners, one hundred twenty muskets, twenty rifles, two casks of ammunition, and several barrels of food.[4] As far as Colonel Pearson was concerned, this escalation in enemy activities only confirmed his determination that the American position at Ogdensburg needed to be permanently neutralized as soon as possible. However, as he could not contravene Sir George Prevost's injunction against engaging in offensive warfare, he sought to gain the appropriate approvals.

Only days later, on February 21st, and to the surprise of everyone, Sir George Prevost himself arrived at Prescott, accompanying a supply column of sleighs. His mission, taken in the depth of winter, was no casual journey; instead it was being made as an urgently needed measure to quell the growing criticism of General Sheaffe's administration of Upper Canada. In addition, Prevost wanted to make a personal assessment of Sheaffe's plan to completely revise the militia system of Upper Canada and establish a series of full-time militia units, including a troop of Provincial Light Cavalry, a troop of Provincial Artillery Drivers, battery companies of Provincial artillery, and, most importantly, three battalions of a new "Incorporated" Militia infantry.

Discussing the current American offensive activities, Prevost heard out Colonel Pearson's request to attack Ogdensburg, but replied by reaffirming his position that no offensive actions were to take place that might disturb the status quo with the Americans. Prevost also notified Colonel Pearson that he was transferring him to Kingston to take over command of that important post, as part of the reorganization Prevost was undertaking among the upper echelon military command in Upper Canada. Pearson's replacement, Major "Red" George Macdonell, of the Glengarry Light Infantry, was appointed effective immediately — as Pearson would be accompanying Prevost when he left the following morning.

Conscious that the Americans had probably received intelligence of his arrival with the supply column and might attack the convoy, Prevost chose to leave early in the morning and without fanfare. As a diversion, Major Macdonell was directed to exercise and parade his troops on the ice-covered St Lawrence River — a practice well established by the British once the weather had created this natural parade ground.

Following orders, Macdonell turned out the garrison for the "demonstration" at dawn. However, once the convoy of sleighs was well on its way, instead of recalling the troops and dismissing his men, Macdonell decided to implement the plan of attack previously developed by Colonel Pearson and take

Two views from the 1813 earthen ramparts of Fort Wellington at Prescott. The existing central blockhouse is a post-war construction. The far bank, beyond the St. Lawrence River, is the United States, clearly indicating the fort's strategic position in controlling waterborne traffic upon the river.

The "Stockade Barracks" at Prescott. Built in 1810, this house was taken over by the military at the start of the war and subsequently saw service as a regimental barracks, food and clothing storehouse, and military hospital.

his chances over the official reaction. Forming his force into two columns around 7:00 a.m., Macdonell ordered his men to advance in rapid time across the intervening span of the river to attack Ogdensburg and the hopefully unprepared American garrison.[*5]

On the American side of the river no serious consideration had been given to mounting an attack on Prevost or the convoy, and in keeping with the bitterly cold weather only the sentries were outside, manning their lonely and frigid duty posts. As the light of day improved, the sight of the British troops parading up and down on the river ice below their fort was nothing out of the ordinary and therefore elicited no immediate sense of alarm. However, this calm was soon shattered as the two

ESTIMATE OF FORCES, BATTLE OF OGDENSBURG, FEBRUARY 22, 1813[5]

American

First U.S. Rifle Regiment (Captain Forsyth), est. 250 all ranks
Albany Volunteer Militia (Captain Kellog), est. 100–200 all ranks
Volunteer militia from Ogdensburg district, est. 50–100 all ranks
Estimated Total, 350–500 all ranks

British

Right (west) Column (Captain John Jenkins)
Glengarry Light Infantry Fencible Regiment (Captain McMillan), 75 all ranks
Dundas Militia Regiment (Captain Ault), 70 all ranks
Artillery (Ensign McKay [GLI]), (Ensign Kerr [Dundas Militia]), est. 20 all ranks

Left (East) Column (Major George McDonell)
8th (King's) Regiment (Captain Eustace), 120 all ranks
Royal Newfoundland Regiment (Captain Le Lievre), 40 all ranks
Dundas Militia Regiment (Colonel Fraser), 200 all ranks
Artillery (Lieutenant Gaugreben [Royal Engineers]), est. 30 all ranks
Estimated Total: 500 all ranks

strong enemy columns rapidly closed upon the American positions. Hearing the alarm sounded by the sentries, the Americans scrambled to dress and man their positions before they were overrun.

Out on the river, the main (left) British column, under Major Macdonell, looked to reach land and move around the village in order to press their attack on the American vulnerable right (northeast) flank. Moving with only minor difficulty through some shallow snowdrifts, and under relatively light fire, the infantry in this column reached the American shore in time to see the sentries beating a hasty retreat through the village. Without waiting for his artillery support, which was having a more difficult and slower crossing, Macdonell led his men through the streets, rapidly quelling any signs of opposition from enemy troops and civilians hiding in the buildings. They also overran the artillery positions stationed on that side of the community.

Meanwhile, Captain John Jenkins' (right) column encountered snowdrifts along the American shoreline that hampered the advance of the infantry and entirely blocked the close support of the artillery pieces on sleighs. Moving down the frozen river, they came under a point-blank fire from no less than seven U.S. artillery pieces and up to two hundred of Forsyth's riflemen, garrisoning the community's small fort stockade. This inflicted a significant number of casualties upon the attackers, including Captain Jenkins, who had an arm amputated by the direct impact of artillery "grapeshot." Continuing to advance and urging his men on, Jenkins was hit yet again, incapacitating him entirely. Under this withering and accurate fire, the column faltered and then withdrew toward Prescott. Here they were rallied and advanced again in support of Macdonell's column, which by then had taken full control of the village and were calling for Forsyth and his men to surrender. Refusing this demand, Forsyth fired his remaining artillery as a final show of defiance before making a hasty retreat with his unwounded men through the fort's rear gate, heading for the nearby woods and then for Sackets Harbor. Left behind were a number of detachments of local militia and the wounded, so that following a mopping-up operation within the various buildings, the final American casualty count was estimated at over fifty men.[6] In addition, a substantial total of ordnance, arms, accoutrements, and supplies also fell into British hands. So voluminous was the total that it took most of the following day to transport it all across the river. Unfortunately, in addition to the legitimate official spoils of victory, some looting of civilian houses in the village also took place. To the credit of the attackers, once this became known to the various officers they went to some lengths to retrieve items "acquired" by their men for return to their legitimate owners. However, nothing could be done about the looting that was confirmed as being done by the retreating American troops or opportunistic members of the local American civilian population. In an interesting sidebar to this event, there are also strong indications that some of the women from Prescott took advantage of the British victory to engage in what today might be colloquially termed a "five-finger discount, cross-border shopping expedition," as a number were subsequently witnessed returning across the river to Prescott during the course of the following day, bearing various sized bundles of items.

ESTIMATE OF CASUALTIES, BATTLE OF OGDENSBURG, FEBRUARY 22, 1813[6]

British

Regulars
Killed: 6 other ranks
Wounded: 3 officers, 9 other ranks

Militias
Killed: 2 rank and file
Wounded: 4 officers, 16 other ranks

American

All Regiments
Killed: estimate of 20–26 all ranks
Wounded and Prisoners: 4 officers, 70 other ranks

With the military garrison subdued and emptied of its valuable weapons and supplies, the fortifications and military warehouses at Ogdensburg were set alight, as were two gunboats and the frozen-in armed schooners *Niagara* and *Dolphin*. Returning to Prescott, Major Macdonell forwarded his official report to Kingston for Sir George Prevost to read and react to.

Upon receipt of Macdonell's report, Sir George was placed in an awkward position. The attack had been undertaken against his openly expressed verbal directions, and even against a letter written after he had departed Prescott. On the other hand, it had resulted in a resounding victory. To now criticize or censure Macdonell for disobedience of orders would only be seen as "sour grapes" and reflect badly on his own position and authority to control his subordinates. He therefore chose to turn a blind eye to this insubordination in his official public release on the action:

> The Commander of the Forces was induced to authorize this attack, not by any means as an act of wanton aggression … but as one of just and necessary retaliation for that which was recently made on the British settlement of Brockville by a party from Ogdensburg … and in announcing its result, His Excellency feels much pleasure in publically expressing his entire approbation of the gallantry and judgment with which it appears to have been conducted….[7]

He also altered the phrasing of Macdonell's official report to create a new version that was forwarded to London, implying that the initiative was, in fact, authorized by him.

> Bulletin No. 46, Sir George Prevost to Earl Bathurst, London … I have the honour of transmitting to Your Lordship the report which Major Macdonnel of the Glengarry Light Infantry Fencibles has made to me of the spirited manner in which he carried into execution my orders on this occasion.[8]

Macdonell was officially "off the hook" and soon became the hero of the hour as the leader of the raid. Unfortunately, no credit was subsequently given to the true architect of the victory, Colonel Pearson — for it was entirely due to his training and preparation of the troops, his design of the plan of action, and his determination to eliminate Ogdensburg as a threat that preserved the slender vital-supply lifeline that linked Lower and Upper Canada.

In contrast, the American reaction to the attack was dramatic and panic stricken. At Sackets Harbor the whole of the local militias were called out and ordered to construct new earthworks and extensive lines of abattis around the base to fend off an anticipated immediate British attack. Regular troops at Plattsburg were rushed overland in sleighs to Sackets to enlarge the garrison, and even Major General Dearborn and the new naval commander Commodore Isaac Chauncey hastened to that post to prepare for the expected onslaught. When this attack failed to materialize, however, instead of standing down his forces, Dearborn decided to implement his invasion plan against Upper Canada, starting from Sackets Harbor. In part, this was from having some of the required troops already in position, but also because the populace of Ogdensburg had raised a hue and cry with the state and federal governments. Far from accepting the British attack as an inevitable result of the international conflict, they blamed Brown and Forsyth's aggressions and the military policies of the government for causing their distressed plight and demanded that no replacement garrison be installed in their community.

Despite the strategic importance of Ogdensburg as the principal point at which the Americans could effectively cut the British supply line to Upper Canada, the upcoming state elections forced the American government to acquiesce to the citizen's demands that for the remainder of the war no significant American military presence garrisoned Ogdensburg. In fact, later accounts report that within weeks, conditions had returned to an almost pre-war state of mutual neutrality between the two communities. Citizens of Prescott continued to shop in Ogdensburg and U.S. civilians were entertained as guests in several prominent local Canadian houses. In addition, extensive and lucrative private agreements were made by the British Army commissariat for the purchase of American cattle and other goods to feed the troops billeted in and around Prescott.

CHAPTER 3

Setting the Pendulum in Motion

In Washington the new secretary of war, John Armstrong, saw the New Year in by attempting to rejuvenate the American war effort. The military staff was reorganized and a system of "Rules and Regulations" was issued to the corps of officers, outlining their duties and responsibilities. In addition, a new cadre of generals were appointed to spearhead the spring campaign season.

Despite these changes, the public backlash from the disasters of the previous year was already threatening the incumbent pro-war Republican administration in the forthcoming April elections for New York State. Consequently the news of new defeats at Frenchtown in the west and Ogdensburg on the St. Lawrence corridor, put Armstrong under intense pressure to produce a positive electoral response to the administration's war policies. He therefore implemented an urgent and intensive schedule of shipbuilding at Sackets Harbor, pumping vast sums of money into the local economy and creating an industrial infrastructure with the goal of simultaneously gaining votes and creating a fleet of vessels that would ensure control of Lake Ontario. In addition, he decided that the new campaign would begin with a two-pronged infantry attack against Upper Canada through the Kingston and Niagara corridors. In a letter to General Dearborn, dated February 10, 1813, Armstrong stated that his immediate goal was to have a combined naval and land force of over 4,000 men eliminate the British fleet at Kingston and take control of Lake Ontario. This invasion force would then move on York (now Toronto) to seize the official capital of Upper Canada. At the same time, a second force of over 3,000 troops would be collected at Buffalo with orders to subdue the British defences on that frontier before pressing westward to cut off Proctor and, after linking up with the new forces being assembled for an attack from the west under Major General Harrison, retake the Michigan Territory and the Detroit River.[1]

However, almost as soon as preparations to implement the new strategy began, Commodore

Image from J. L. Thompson, Historical Sketches of the Late War between the United States and Great Britain, 1816.

Commander of the U.S. naval fleet on Lake Ontario, Commodore Isaac Chauncey.

Isaac Chauncey proposed changes to the plan. Arguing that Kingston was too heavily defended to be attacked without heavy cost, Chauncey proposed that York (Toronto) be targeted first, followed by an all-out invasion upon the Niagara frontier — but in this alteration he was overruled. Unfortunately, a combination of poor weather conditions, difficulties assembling the necessary supplies, weapons, and troops, and a late spring thaw effectively delayed the planned attack on Kingston until it became impractical, and Chauncey's plan was hurriedly adopted as the primary alternative.

The assault force began embarking on April 20th, and after three days of intense effort was ready to proceed, only to see the weather worsen. Overruling the advice of his naval commanders, Dearborn ordered the heavily overburdened American fleet to set sail, only to encounter a severe storm that forced the ships to come about and run back to Sackets Harbor for shelter. During the next two days the troops were either forced to endure being locked below decks in cramped unsanitary conditions, or sit exposed on the open decks under a drenching rain and below-normal temperatures. When the weather finally cleared, the fleet sailed on April 25, 1813.[*2] Major General Dearborn held overall command, while under him Commodore Isaac Chauncey led the naval squadron and Brigadier General Zebulon Pike commanded the landing forces.

Commander of the American landing forces at the Battle of York, Brigadier General Zebulon Pike.

AMERICAN INVASION FORCE, APRIL 1813[2]

Naval Force

Madison (Lieutenant Commander Elliott), 24 guns, ship
Oneida (Lieutenant Commander Woolsey), 18 guns, brig
Fair American (Lieutenant Chauncey), 2 guns, schooner
Hamilton (Lieutenant McPherson), 9 guns, schooner
Governor Tompkins (Lieutenant Brown), 6 guns, schooner
Conquest (Mr. Mallaby), 3 guns, schooner
Asp (Lieutenant Smith), 2 guns, sloop
Pert (Lieutenant Adams), 3 guns, schooner
Julia (Mr. Trant), 2 guns, schooner
Growler (Mr. Mix), 5 guns, schooner
Ontario (Mr. Stevens), 2 guns, schooner
Scourge (Mr. Osgood), 10 guns, schooner
Lady of the Lake (Mr. Flynn), 1 gun, schooner
Raven (Mr. Bowers), 1 gun, schooner
Mounting a total of 88 cannon, with 700 crew

Landing Force

Sixth Regiment (Colonel Simonds), 300 all ranks
Thirteenth Regiment (Ensign Dwight), 40-man detachment attached to Fourteenth Regiment
Fourteenth Regiment (Captain Grindage), 95 all ranks
Fifteenth Regiment (Major King), 458 all ranks
Sixteenth Regiment (Colonel Pearce), 290 all ranks
Twenty-First Regiment (Lieutenant Colonel Ripley), 133 all ranks
First Rifle Regiment (Major Forsyth), est. 175 all ranks
Third Artillery Regiment (Lieutenant Fanning), est. 80 all ranks
Light Artillery Regiment (Major Eustis), est. 80 all ranks
New York State Volunteer Militia (Colonel McClure), est. 125 all ranks

As Chauncey had proposed, their destination was York, capital of Upper Canada and the site of a small dockyard that was building a new vessel, the *Sir Isaac Brock*, for the British flotilla. This ship was scheduled to mount no less than twenty-six 32-pounder short-barrelled carronades as her main broadside armament and two pairs of 18-pounder long guns as bow and stern chasers. As the next largest British vessel, the *Royal George*, carried only twenty of these carronades, while the largest American vessel then afloat, the *Madison*, also had twenty-six carronades, the *Sir Isaac Brock* therefore represented a major threat to the Americans and a valuable prize for the taking. In addition, the *Duke of Gloucester* and *General Hunter* were undergoing repairs at York. If these two ships were also captured intact they would greatly augment the American naval powerbase on Lake Ontario.

Under changing winds and choppy swells, the American fleet arrived within sight of the town on the evening of Monday the 26th — causing the garrison at Fort York to sound the alarm guns as a signal that war was descending on their quiet bayside community.

Unfortunately, the fortifications of Fort York were completely inadequate to the task of fending off an enemy attack. In fact, the fort could be better described as a small supply depot, defended by mediocre blockhouses, loopholed barracks, dilapidated

The antiquated Cromwell-era cannon used at the battle of York, now on display at the Fort York historic site in Toronto.

Toronto Reference Library, JRR 15211.

The Sir Isaac Brock, Owen Staples, artist, date unknown. An impression of the incomplete *Sir Isaac Brock* on the stocks at the small shipyard at York in 1813. The partially dismantled *Duke of Gloucester* is in the background. The *Brock* was the primary target for capture by the invaders, but deliberately burned by the retreating British during the battle to deny the Americans this valuable prize.

Fort York, S. Streton, artist, circa 1803. The early fort (1793) with the Government House lies inside the low fence (centre left), while the 1813 fort (that the Americans attacked) lies to the right of the flagstaff. The stone magazine (not shown) was built directly into the lakeside embankment, about where the low fence ends at left.

Fort York, S. Streton, artist, circa 1804. A view of Fort York as it would have appeared at the time of the attack in April 1813.

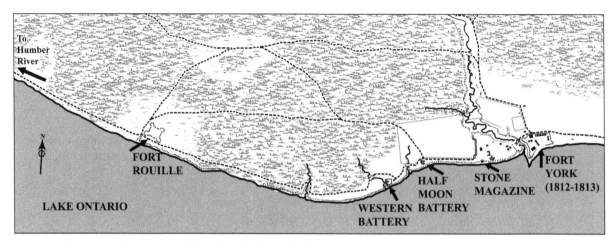

Above and facing: The town of York and its defences in 1813

gun batteries, and antiquated artillery pieces (one of which dated back to the period of Oliver Cromwell, some 150 years earlier!). These derelict antiques had previously been condemned and had their trunnions (elevating swivels) cut off to make them unworkable. However, at the onset of war, these substandard weapons had been resurrected for active use and mounted on makeshift carriages using heavy-duty clamps and straps to hold the barrels in place. The only question was, who would be the first to be killed by these guns, the enemy or their crew? In a similar vein, although additional defensive earthworks and a small battery position had been constructed to the west of the main garrison, protecting the official governmental residence, none were complete or fully

armed with artillery. Finally, although intended to be already afloat, construction of the *Sir Isaac Brock* was seriously behind schedule, due to infighting between the senior officials in charge of the project and the either total incompetence or deliberate malfeasance of the dockyard supervisor, Thomas Plunkett.

THE BATTLE OF YORK, APRIL 27, 1813

At dawn on April 27th, the American fleet began their approach toward land. General Sheaffe expected they would make simultaneous landings on both flanks of the fort, and in response had detached a battalion company of the 8th (King's) Regiment,

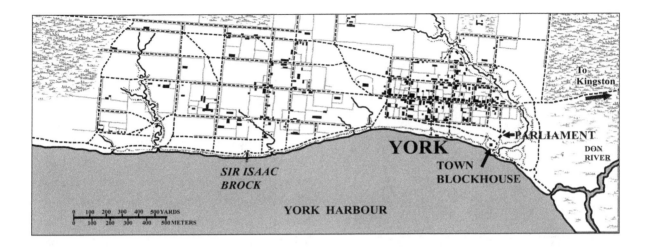

plus detachments of militia to cover his eastern flank, protect the town, and cover his line of communications and retreat to Kingston. The remainder of his troops he held at the fort until the American intentions became clear.[*3] However, pressed by a strengthening wind, the American fleet was blown well west of its planned landing site, into the wide Humber Bay lying beyond a small headland. As a result, they were well beyond the range of any of the fort's guns or detached batteries and would be able to land unopposed. There was also the distinct possibility that, by landing near to the Humber River, the Americans might locate the inland trail that led directly from the river crossing to the north side of York, bypassing all of the established defences that faced the lake.[*4] In response, Sheaffe was forced to improvise a new defensive plan. Recalling his eastern detachments, he sent the bulk of his Embodied Militia, backed by the Glengarry Light Infantry, north to cover the inland road. Beyond that, however, the remainder of the detachments were simply ordered to march toward the projected American landing site and engage the enemy, with no planned strategic or tactical coordination, and, more importantly, no artillery support. Unfortunately, as they advanced along the lakeside trail, these detachments soon came under cannon fire from the American fleet. As a result, some units were forced to detour and wend their way along narrower inland footpaths, thus delaying their commitment against the enemy.

Major General R.H. Sheaffe ("Sheef") in later life. He was fifty years old at the time of the Battle of York. Partially as a result of criticism over his defeat at York, he was later replaced as lieutenant governor of Upper Canada (June 1813), before being eventually recalled to England in August 1813, where he saw out the end of the war.

As the American landing boats approached the shore, to the west of the ruins of the old French trading post Fort Rouillé, only a party of Native warriors were in place under the cover of the treeline. Opening fire, they inflicted heavy casualties amongst the tightly packed Americans until increasing numbers of Forsyth's riflemen landed on their flank and forced them to retreat through the woods. At this point, the grenadier company from the 8th (King's) Regiment arrived at the landing zone and, although already vastly outnumbered, immediately engaged the enemy troops with a tight volley. Replying in kind, the Americans pressed forward, leading to hand-to-hand fighting in the shallows and along the beach. Within the space of a few moments, the "King's" detachment had lost some forty-six men killed and a further thirty wounded, including their commander, Captain Neal McNeale. Without additional reinforcements, the few surviving defenders began a fighting retreat against the American advance guard, while the succeeding waves of Americans consolidated their bridgehead before commencing their advance toward the British garrison.

Reaching a lakeside clearing at the site of the derelict Fort Rouillé, the Americans came up against the hastily assembled British line, composed of companies of the Royal Newfoundland Regiment, the 8th (King's) Regiment, one company of the newly formed Incorporated Militia, and, as the action continued, the Glengarry Light Infantry, who had left the Embodied Militia positions and marched to the

GARRISON FORCES, FORT YORK, APRIL 1813[*3]

Garrison Commander: Lieutenant Colonel Heathcote, Royal Newfoundland Regiment

8th (King's) Regiment: Grenadier Company (Captain McNeale), 29 other ranks

No. 3 Company (Captain Eustace), 150 other ranks (plus detachments from companies 6, 7, and 9, est. 50 other ranks)

49th Regiment (detachments under N.C.O.'s command), 20 other ranks

Royal Newfoundland Regiment (Lieutenant Colonel Heathcote), 92 other ranks

Glengarry Light Infantry (Captain McPherson), 56 other ranks

Royal Artillery (detached from Captain Holcroft's battery), 13 gunners

Flank Company 1st York Militia (Major Wilmot), est. 125 other ranks

Flank Company 3rd York Militia (Lieutenant Colonel Chewett), est. 200 other ranks

Flank Company 1st Durham Militia (Captain Burn), est. 15 other ranks

Volunteer Battalion of Incorporated Militia (Captain Jarvie), 20 other ranks

Volunteer Battalion of Incorporated Militia Artillery (Captain Jarvis), 20 gunners

Native allies volunteers (Major Givins), est. 50–80 warriors

Volunteers from the town and dockyard, est. 300–400 men

(*N.B.* Due to the piecemeal involvement of units and the fact that General Sheaffe subsequently reported his numbers without access to any documentation [it being captured], plus the fact that he had to justify an embarrassing military and strategic loss to his superiors, Sheaffe's numbers have always been deemed suspect. Recent investigations have revealed that it is now almost certain Sheaffe significantly underreported the numbers of his own force, perhaps by as much as 25 percent, to cover his failure.)

AMERICAN INVASION ORDER, ISSUED APRIL 25, 1813[*4]

Leading Wave
Light Troops, Riflemen (Major Forsyth)

2nd Wave
1st Brigade (Major King)
Riflemen detachments from Fifteenth/Sixteenth Regiments (Captain Walworth)
2 artillery pieces (Captain Brooks)
Reserve: 1st Brigade (Major Swan)

3rd Wave (Reserve)
Artillery and covering infantry (Major Eustis)
Volunteers (Colonel McClure)
Twenty-First Regiment (Colonel Ripley)
Fifteenth Regiment, detachment (Captain Steel)

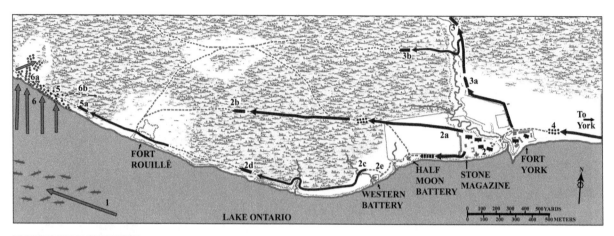

THE BATTLE OF YORK.

The Initial American Landings and Countermoves, April 27, 1813 (circa 5:30–8:00 a.m.)

1. The American flotilla (1) arrives off York, but strong winds push them past the entrance to the shelter of the York Bay and into the open waters of Humber Bay, beyond the range of the defending batteries at Fort York, the Half-Moon Battery, and Western Battery.

2. General Sheaffe gathers his troops at Fort York (2) but fails to establish any coordinated response to the American attack. Units move out independently from Fort York toward the American landing by either taking one of the inland trails (to avoid being fired on by the American ships) (2a, 2b) or using the lakefront trail (2c, 2d). Captain Jarvis's Incorporated Militia artillery detachment man guns in the Western Battery (2e).

3. Canadian embodied militia units (3) move north of the town to secure the main communication road leading west and await further orders, followed shortly afterward by the Glengarry Light Infantry (3a). En route, the Glengarry Light Infantry break off and march toward the sounds of gunfire (3b).

4. A detachment of Incorporated Militia under Captain Jarvie (4) arrive at York and march to the fort to join the action.

5. Native allied warriors (5) lead the advance of the units sent to oppose the American landing, followed by a company of the 8th (Kings) Regiment (5a).

6. The American advance force (6) lands under fire, initially from the Natives and later from the 8th (Kings), resulting in fierce close-quarter and hand-to-hand fighting. With the support of additional troops landing on the British-Native flank (6a), the Americans overwhelm the defenders and consolidate a bridgehead, while the scattered defenders retreat toward Fort Rouillé (6b).

42

sound of the guns. For over an hour the action fluctuated across the clearing, with both sides pressing to gain an advantage. However, as additional American reinforcements joined the action, the balance of firepower shifted in favour of the Americans. Eventually, without reinforcements and taking increasing numbers of casualties, the defenders were forced to break off and make yet another slow fighting retreat, this time to the Western Battery. Here they expected they would be reinforced by the previously detached Embodied Militia units. However, apart from Captain Jarvie's company of Incorporated Militia, which had already taken casualties in the fighting at Fort Rouillé, no additional help was forthcoming. Once the Americans came within range, the troops that had crowded inside the Western Battery opened fire and another heavy exchange of shooting began. However, moments later, the accidental explosive ignition of some exposed artillery ammunition wrecked the guns, killing or injuring over thirty individuals and, despite some immediate efforts to bring it back into action, effectively rendered the position untenable. The only remaining line of defence was the incomplete earthen wall and dilapidated wooden stockade of Fort York. However, to counter this possibility the American fleet moved up directly south of the stockade and began firing, systematically demolishing everything in sight and making exposed movement by the defenders impossible. General Sheaffe, realizing the day was lost, ordered a general retreat toward the town by his remaining regular troops. Determined to deny the Americans the contents of the fort's sturdy stone ammunition magazine, which by one estimate contained over 30,000 pounds of powder and explosive shells, General Sheaffe ordered the magazine's deliberate detonation. Built into the lakeside embankment, directly below the Government House, this storehouse was partially buried under a mound of earth and heavy timbers, with only its open front face being left exposed. It was also directly south of the shallow stream bed, located just on the north side of the fort, that had been detailed for the assembly of the Canadian militia units at the onset of the battle. With the retreat and explosion at the Western Battery several detachments of the militia, including those of the Incorporated Militia, had gone back to their original assembly point to reform their units and look for further orders. Unfortunately, Sheaffe neglected to send any orders or notification to this militia location. As a result, the unsuspecting militiamen were left behind, only a matter of two hundred yards (183 meters) from the impending detonation.

Meanwhile, considering the day as won, General Pike was marshalling his troops into a column upon the open ground to the southwest of the fort and in clear view of the exposed front face of

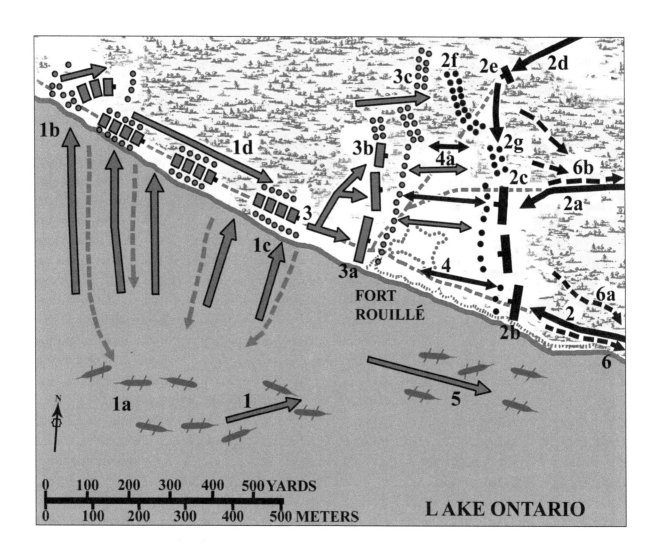

2f 2e 2d
3c
1b
1d
3b 4a 2g
6b
3 2c
1c 2a
3a 4 6a
FORT
ROUILLÉ 2
2b
6
N
1a 1
5

0   100   200   300   400   500 YARDS
0   100   200   300   400   500 METERS

LAKE ONTARIO

THE BATTLE AT FORT ROUILLÉ
(circa 8:00–9:30 a.m.)

1. In support of their landings, part of the U.S. flotilla (1) begins to sail east, firing onshore at any target of opportunity, while the remainder (1a) continue to land troops along a wide front (1b, 1c). Onshore, American units press forward along the lakefront trail (1d).

2. British units (2, 2a) advance toward the clearing near Fort Rouillé. Upon arrival, they establish a rough line of defence (2b, 2c). Captain Jarvie's company of Incorporated Militia arrives (2d) and is initially placed in-line on the right flank (2e) in support of the Glengarry Light Infantry (2f). Subsequently the company is redeployed into an open skirmish order to act as light troops and close the gap in the British right wing (2g).

3. Reaching the Fort Rouillé clearing and seeing the British line, the American units (3) form line-of-battle (3a, 3b) with the rifle units and militia on their left flank (3c).

4. Close-quarter fighting fluctuates across the open clearing (4, 4a).

5. U.S. vessels (5) move alongside the British-Canadian position and fire into their flank, causing significant casualties.

6. Overwhelmed by U.S. numbers and firepower, the British-Canadian units begin a fighting withdrawal toward the Western Battery and Fort York (6, 6a, 6b).

the fort's magazine. Expecting Sheaffe would make a formal surrender, as the royal standard still flew over the Government House, Pike and his men relaxed in their assured victory. Suddenly, the earth quaked and a gigantic smoky fireball erupted into the afternoon air, carrying with it masses of stone, metal, and timber from the exploded magazine and its contents, as well as pieces of bedrock from the surrounding ground. Channelled and focused by the fort's earthen ramparts toward the exposed front of the magazine, the initial concussion of the blast wave swept over the open ground to the west of the fort, literally blowing the American troops off their feet and onto the ground, rupturing eardrums, and invisibly inflicting severe internal injuries upon many of the troops. Seconds later large chunks of the debris began to crash to earth amongst the exposed American troops, causing additional havoc in the previously regimented columns. Over 250 men were immediately killed or subsequently died from the effects of this blast, including General Pike, who was struck by a large stone fragment and died shortly thereafter. Even aboard the American fleet offshore the explosion caused damage and casualties as debris flew over 500 yards (457 meters) from the point of detonation. Interestingly, although significantly closer to the source of the explosion, the forgotten Canadian militiamen were partially protected by the fort's earthworks and the gully of the

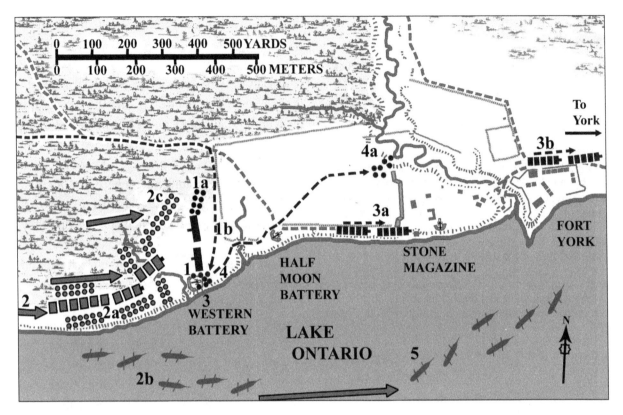

stream bed in which they stood. As a result, they suffered fewer numbers of injured from the direct blast, but did incur several casualties as a result of the subsequent falling debris.[*5]

Expecting a British counterattack, the deputy American commander, Colonel Cromwell Pearce, only rallied his shocked troops with some difficulty. But Sheaffe failed to take advantage of the moment and continued his retreat toward the town,

burning the *Sir Isaac Brock* on the stocks, as well as warehouses containing a quantity of valuable naval supplies destined for General Proctor on the Detroit frontier. Sheaffe then continued his retreat through the town and out onto the Kingston Road. Even the arrival of additional reinforcements (the Light company of the 8th [King's] Regiment) failed to persuade Sheaffe to make a further stand and it was left to Lieutenant Colonel William Chewett

THE BRITISH RETREAT AND EXPLOSION AT THE WESTERN BATTERY (circa 9:30–11:00 a.m.)

1. British forces, having made a fighting retreat to the Western Battery, establish a new line of defence (1, 1a). Captain Jarvie's company arrives and enters the battery (1b).

2. The main American force advances along the lakefront trail (2, 2a), supported by the firepower of their fleet on their right (2b) and riflemen on their left (2c).

3. Fire from the British line and Western Battery (3) halts the American advance until an accidental explosion inside the battery causes serious casualties among the defenders and makes the position untenable. Following the explosion, some defending units retreat toward Fort York (3a), while other detachments begin an evacuation toward York (3b).

4. Captain Jarvie's and Lieutenant Jarvis's companies (4) evacuate the Western Battery and move into the shelter of the creek bed lying north of Government House and the stone magazine (4a).

5. American fleet vessels (5) move into the York harbour and begin a bombardment of the Fort York defences, as well as firing on any targets of opportunity.

The stone magazine at Historic Fort York, built in 1813/1814 to replace the exploded magazine. While the previous building was partially buried into the lakeside embankment, this structure is of a similar size, design, and construction to the one destroyed at the battle.

Image courtesy of the U.S. Naval Academy Museum, Annapolis, MD.

The only available image (from 1913) of the Royal Standard captured by the Americans at York in 1813 and still in their hands as of 2012.

and Major William Allen of the 3rd York Embodied Militia, accompanied by the local firebrand clergyman, Reverend John Strachan, to treat with the Americans for the terms of surrender. Frustrated in their attempts to lay hands on the *Sir Isaac Brock* and having suffered so severely from the explosion, the Americans dealt harshly with the Canadian

THE MAGAZINE EXPLODES AT FORT YORK (circa 11:30 a.m.–12:30 p.m.)

1. The American force (1), considering the day won, advances to the west of Fort York and, after sending pickets forward to cover their front (1a), begin to form units in preparation for an expected formal surrender of the fort and town (1b).

2. A detachment of British troops rig and detonate the main stone magazine to deny it to the Americans (2).

3. The resultant blast (3) and explosion debris causes significant casualties within the assembled American columns. Lesser degrees of damage and injury are also inflicted aboard vessels of the American fleet (3a), within Fort York (3b), and among the ranks of Jarvie and Jarvis' forgotten units of Canadian militia in the garrison creek bed on the north side of the Government House (3c).

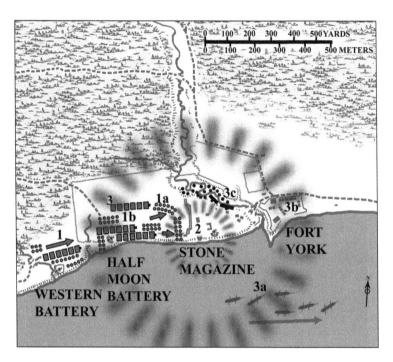

negotiators and imposed strong terms for the surrender of the town.

During the next few days, the Americans, abetted by local pro-American sympathizers, emptied the military storehouses and major private warehouses around the town and, despite previous official American assurances, also looted private homes. In addition, the main government and public buildings were ransacked and burned, including the Upper Canada Parliament, inciting Strachan to

call upon Dearborn for better treatment and compliance with the terms of the surrender. Eventually, on May 2nd, the American forces began to reembark on their augmented fleet, taking the *Duke of Gloucester* was as a prize, while the *General Hunter*, deemed unfit for sea, was burned.

At dawn on June 2nd, Commodore Chauncey and General Dearborn both set sail for Fort Niagara, but by noon a return of storms and adverse winds trapped the remaining vessels of the American fleet

OFFICIAL ESTIMATE OF CASUALTIES, BATTLE OF YORK, APRIL 27, 1813[5]

American (Regulars and Militias)

Killed in battle:	1 officer, 2 musicians, 9 other ranks
Wounded in battle:	2 officers, 29 other ranks
Killed by Explosion:	1 brigadier general, 1 officer, 33 other ranks
Wounded by Explosion:	14 officers, 1 musician, 205 other ranks
Killed on fleet:	1 officer, 1 seaman
Wounded on fleet:	11 seamen

British Regulars

Killed:	2 officer, 1 sergeant major, 1 drummer, 34 other ranks
Wounded:	23 other ranks
Wounded/Prisoners:	29 other ranks
Prisoners:	1 sergeant major, 40 other ranks

Canadian Fencibles (G.L.I. and Royal Newfoundland Regiment)

Killed:	1 drummer, 13 other ranks
Wounded:	3 officers, 13 other ranks
Wounded Prisoners:	112 other ranks
Prisoners:	2 other ranks
Missing:	5 other ranks

Canadian Militias

Killed:	number unknown, at least 4
Wounded:	number unknown, at least 6
Prisoners:	38 officers, 227 other ranks

Royal Artillery

Killed:	3 gunners
Wounded:	7 gunners
Prisoners:	5 gunners
Missing:	7 gunners

Provincial Navy

Prisoners:	4 officers, 1 clerk, 1 boatswain, 15 naval artificiers

Native Allies

Killed:	Number unknown, at least 5
Wounded:	Number unknown, at least 8

(*N.B.* The American estimate of British losses in the action amounted to 200 killed and wounded and 550 prisoners, including 50 regulars.)

at York, their holds and decks jammed with captured goods, wounded, and seasick troops. Once again the men had to suffer the miseries of waiting until the weather cleared on the 8th, when they finally set sail for the Niagara frontier. Behind them, the traumatized and angry citizens of York began to reclaim their lives, while condemning Sheaffe for abandoning them at their moment of crisis.

From a political point of view, the Americans had finally scored a legitimate victory, although at a heavy human cost. Strategically, they had gained the upper hand in the season's campaigning. Sheaffe had retreated to Kingston and, fearing a further American attack, had begun fortifying the waterfront of the town and constructing a

Image courtesy of the Legislative Assembly of Ontario.

The Parliamentary mace, the symbol of royal authority, captured by the Americans in 1813 and eventually returned to Canadian hands in 1934.

Toronto Reference Library, JRR 1084.

A later impression of the Upper Canada Parliament Buildings, burnt by the Americans in April 1813.

new fort on the hilltop at Point Henry, overlooking the town and harbour. He was unable to transport any reinforcements or supplies directly to the Niagara or Detroit frontiers. On the other hand, although General Dearborn was free to manoeuvre at will, once his troops arrived at Fort Niagara they found that although Dearborn had been there for nearly a week, almost nothing had been done to prepare any accommodations or food for their arrival. Exhausted and sickly, Dearborn's disgruntled troops were left with no option but to set-to to build their camps and begin the process of preparing for the planned invasion of the Niagara frontier.

York, Upper Canada, E. Hale, artist, circa 1804. The quiet bayside community of York, prior to the war. The Upper Canada Parliament Buildings and town blockhouse are visible in the distance (right). Note the proximity of the uncleared forest, dominating man's attempt at settlement during this period.

CHAPTER 4

Line Versus Line:
The Battle of Fort George, May 27, 1813

Learning of the fall of York, Brigadier General John Vincent, commander of the British forces on the Niagara, was painfully aware that his army was effectively cut off from reinforcement and support. In addition, his main reserves of food, ammunition, weapons, etc., previously thought safe at York, were now in the hands of the enemy. Knowing he would be the next target, Vincent's disposable defence force consisted of just over 1,000 regular troops and militia, stationed across over thirty miles (50 kilometers) of frontier.[*1] On May 8th the main American fleet appeared and landed the regiments used in the capture of York to the east of Fort Niagara, out of range of the British guns.

Although ill and effectively unable to fulfil his duties, General Dearborn continued to act as commander of the American army. However, despite the significant number of troops already assembled around Fort Niagara, Dearborn felt that it was important to augment this force. He therefore sent orders to Oswego for 700 men of that garrison (under Colonel Winfield Scott) to march for the Niagara frontier. In addition, Brigadier General Morgan Lewis was ordered to transfer a sizeable portion of the troops stationed around Buffalo to Fort Niagara. Finally, Commodore Chauncey was directed to return to Sackets Harbor and, after offloading the goods captured at York, embark additional reinforcements, artillery, and supplies for delivery to the Niagara to complete the invasion force.

Leaving the vessels, *Governor Tompkins* and *Conquest*, as guards off the mouth of the Niagara River, Chauncey sailed back to Sackets Harbor with

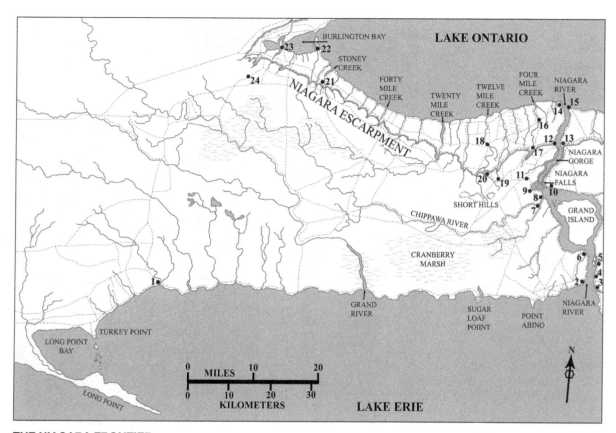

THE NIAGARA FRONTIER

1. Port Dover
2. Fort Erie [Fort Erie]
3. Buffalo
4. Black Rock
5. U.S. Naval Yard on Scajaquada Creek
6. Frenchman's Creek
7. Weishoun's
8. [Fort Chippawa]
9. Bridgewater Mills
10. Fort Schlosser
11. Lundy's Lane Hilltop
12. Queenston
13. Lewiston
14. Newark (Niagara-on-the-Lake) [Fort George, Fort Mississauga]
15. [Fort Niagara]
16. Crossroads (Virgil)
17. St. Davids
18. Shipman's Corners (St. Catharines)
19. Beaver Dams
20. De Cou (DeCew) Mill
21. Stoney Creek
22. King's Head Inn
23. Burlington Heights (Hamilton)
24. Ancaster

BRITISH / CANADIAN FORCES, NIAGARA FRONTIER, MAY 1813[1]

Fort Erie

Royal Artillery, 10 gunners
Royal Artillery Drivers, 1 other ranks
41st Regiment, 178 other ranks
Royal Newfoundland Regiment, 95 other ranks

Putnam's

Glengarry Light Infantry, 109 other ranks
Royal Artillery, 2 gunners

Frenchman's Creek

Royal Artillery, 8 other ranks
49th Regiment, 53 other ranks

Chippawa

Royal Artillery Drivers, 5 other ranks
8th (King's) Regiment, 84 other ranks
49th Regiment, 92 other ranks

Detached Batteries

Royal Artillery, 8 other ranks
41st Regiment, 33 other ranks

Fort George

Royal Artillery, 30 other ranks
8th (Kings) Regiment, 214 other ranks
41st Regiment, 165 other ranks
49th Regiment, 255 other ranks
Captain Runchey's Company of Colour, 28 other ranks
Militia detachments, 172 other ranks
Artificers, 88 other ranks
Total: 1623 other ranks

the bulk of his fleet, only to find that once again the garrison was in an extreme state of alarm over rumours that the British were preparing to attack from Kingston. As a result, Chauncey deemed it prudent to leave three vessels at Sackets Harbor for its defence, while the remaining ships were despatched in pairs over a number of days, carrying troops under the command of Brigadier General John Chandler.

Chauncey himself did not sail for the Niagara River until May 21st.

Upon Chauncey's arrival, he found that in his absence General Dearborn had overruled his orders and used the *Conquest* and *Governor Tompkins* to transport about a hundred men of the Twelfth Regiment (Captain Morgan) on a raid to the Head-of-the-Lake. Their goal was to destroy both the

The King's Head, O. Staples, artist, 1910. This later rendition shows the sand bar dividing the western end of Lake Ontario (right) from the harbour of Burlington Bay (left). The building (centre) is the King's Head Tavern, which was burned by the American's during their visit in May 1813.

British supply base at Burlington Heights and the local grain mills west of that position. On May 11th this force had landed on the sand spit that marked the harbour at Burlington Heights and, after driving off a small detachment of militiamen guarding a storehouse, had burned both it and the nearby King's Head Tavern. Intending to advance further, they heard that a force of Canadian militia and Native allies were advancing on their position. They therefore returned to their boats and set sail for Niagara to report their "victory."

Not impressed that Dearborn had counter-manded his directives for the use of *his* ships, Chauncey also found that while land-related preparations for the invasion had been made no one had thought to include acquiring the longboats by which the army could make its landing on the enemy's shore. Chauncey was consequently left with the job of locating the essential craft if the invasion was to take place on time.

Watching the American preparations, Vincent was woefully aware of his precarious position. More

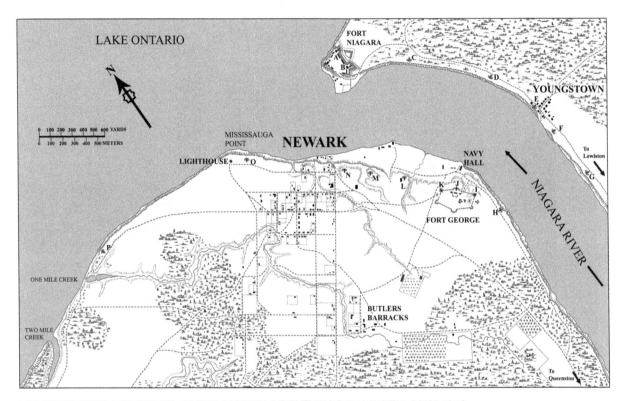

MILITARY EMPLACEMENTS AT THE MOUTH OF THE NIAGARA RIVER, MAY 1813

Key

A, B   U.S. battery positions at Fort Niagara
C to G   U.S. detached riverside batteries.
H   British detached upper riverside battery.
I to K   British battery positions at Fort George.
L to O   British detached lower riverside "Newark" batteries.
P   British detached lakeside battery.

than a third of his regular infantry, half his artillery, and two-thirds of the militia were guarding the southern end of the Niagara River under Lieutenant Colonel Bisshopp. In the centre, below the gorge, the six detached batteries located between Queenston and Fort George all required manning and infantry support in case the Americans attempted a repeat of their October crossing. Finally, at the river mouth, Fort George was still in a "very ruinous and unfinished condition,"[2] as other military priorities had used up the limited resources of men and materiel elsewhere, while the detached batteries fronting the river and lake were all exposed to flanking fire from the American fleet. Only a month earlier Vincent had proposed making a pre-emptive strike on Fort Niagara, to eliminate the then-undermanned American base. However, Sheaffe had vetoed this operation. Now the opportunity had slipped away and Vincent was facing a significantly superior force of land-based troops, fully supported by riverside artillery batteries and a naval flotilla that could land troops anywhere along the Lake Ontario shore in his rear, thus cutting him off from reinforcement or escape.

Without knowing where this enemy blow would fall, Vincent was forced to disperse his command to cover all eventualities. On the right flank Lieutenant Colonel Harvey's troops watched the riverbank between Fort George and Queenston, while on the left flank Lieutenant Colonel Myers supervised the troops stationed at the river mouth and lakefront. Between the two detachments, at Fort George, Vincent held back a reserve of 300 men from the 49th Regiment, plus a number of ad hoc detachments, composed principally of sick and non-combatant troops, in order to move to whichever flank might come under attack. As the threat of invasion intensified, Vincent ordered his troops to be placed on alert each night.

For over a week the men turned out at 2:00 a.m. and remained under arms until daylight revealed that yet another night's sleep had been lost without result. By the night of May 24–25th, the British and Canadian troops were exhausted and nerves were stretched to breaking point. Consequently, when sentries upriver heard noises at the American "Five Mile" meadow they raised the alarm and began firing, which cascaded toward Fort George as the sounds moved downriver. Dawn revealed the sounds to be a small flotilla of lightly manned boats skirting the American shore and making for Fort Niagara. As the boats passed by Fort George, the garrison opened up with five pieces of ordnance. In response, the American riverside batteries retaliated with no less than twenty-five cannon and mortars, deluging the fort with shell and incendiary "hotshot." By noon almost every building inside the fort, as well as the surrounding wooden stockade, was burning fiercely and the artillery crews, although initially attempting to maintain the unequal contest with the American batteries, were soon forced to abandon their posts.

Downriver, the river-mouth batteries had been forced to remain idle, being under orders not to engage the enemy unless directly fired upon, because it was feared that any American shot that missed its target would land upon Newark. As a result, throughout the afternoon sentries watched impotently as boats from the American fleet edged along the Lake Ontario shoreline, making soundings and placing buoys, clearly indicating that the American fleet would place itself in the rear of the British positions to provide fire support for any landings in that quarter. Much of the civilian populace had already evacuated the town in favour of a more secure position some miles inland, including St. Davids, the

Above: *A view of Fort George, Navy Hall and New Niagara, taken from the United States Fort of Old Niagara*, E. Walsh, artist, circa 1805. A detail from a view showing the Canadian bank of the Niagara River at Newark (Niagara-on-the-Lake) in 1805. Fort George and Navy Hall lie to the left, while Newark is to the right.

Right: The modern reconstruction of Fort George, as seen from the American side of the Niagara River.

Facing: The reconstructed officer's mess (top), blockhouse barracks (middle), and earthwork bastions/ditch (bottom) at the Fort George National Historic site.

Crossroads (Virgil), and Shipman's Corners (St. Catharines). Fort George was effectively a gutted wreck and incapable of maintaining any kind of defence, while Lieutenant Colonel Bisshopp's force remained pinned above Niagara Falls in case of any assault on that flank. However, no attack materialized on the 26th due to Commodore Chauncey's inability to collect sufficient longboats to ferry the troops from the ships to the shore, necessitating a delay while additional boats were brought up from further along the lake.

Before dawn on the morning of May 27, 1813, and under the cover of a thick fog, the American fleet rowed out into the lake until they reached a position directly behind the British left flank, between the lighthouse at Mississauga Point and Two Mile Creek, whereupon they anchored to await the dawn. To distract Vincent, the guns of Fort Niagara and the riverside batteries opened a fresh bombardment upon Fort George, persuading the British commander that it was indeed the fort that would be the target of the main American assault. With daylight came a slight breeze, which rolled away the curtain of fog from the lake to reveal the impressive sight of some sixteen sailing vessels stationed across the mouth of the river, their guns targeting the line of British defences and proposed landing ground. Alongside the fleet could be seen three lines of over 130 smaller boats, crammed with infantry.[*3]

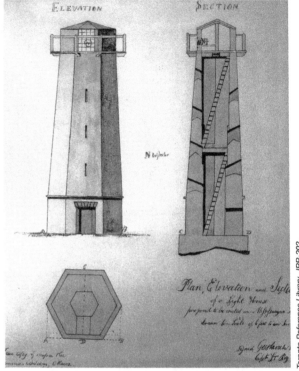

Toronto Reference Library, JRR-202.

Plan for the Point Mississauga Lighthouse, 1804, H.R. Holmden, artist, 1804. In 1813 the lighthouse keeper and his wife tended to the wounded from both sides during the battle for Fort George.

At a signal from the flagship, the larger ships began firing at the exposed shore batteries, while the smaller armed vessels edged inshore to cover the landings. Between them the first wave of twenty landing boats pulled for the shore, packed with over 800 troops and commanded by Lieutenant Colonel

AMERICAN FORCES, BATTLE OF FORT GEORGE, MAY 27, 1813[*3]

***First Wave (Lieutenant Colonel Scott),
est. 900 all ranks***

Sixth/Fifteenth/Sixteenth Regiments (Lieutenant
Colonel Scott)
First Rifle Regiment (Lieutenant Colonel Forsyth)
Fifteenth Regiment (Major Lewis)
Second /Third U.S. Artillery (Colonel Porter),
1 x 3 pounder

***Second Wave (Brigadier General Boyd),
est. 1,600 all ranks***

Second/Third U.S. Artillery (Major Eustis), 4 guns
New York State Volunteer Rifles Regiment
(Lieutenant Colonel McClure)
Sixth Regiment (Colonel Miller)
Fifteenth Regiment (Major King)
Sixteenth Regiment (Colonel Pearce)

***Third Wave (Brigadier General Winder),
est. 1,500 all ranks***

Second/Third U.S. Artillery (Captain Towson), 4 guns
Fifth Regiment (Lieutenant Colonel Milton)
Thirteenth Regiment (Major Huyck)
Fourteenth Regiment (Lieutenant Colonel Boerstler)
Twenty-First Regiment (Colonel Ripley)

***Reserve (Brigadier General Chandler),
est. 1,500 all ranks***

Ninth Regiment (Not known)
Twenty-Third Regiment (Major Armstrong)
Twenty-Fifth Regiment (Major Smith)
U.S. Marines and Seamen
Brigadier General Chandler's Brigade
Colonel Macomb's Corps of Artillery
Estimate, 5500 all ranks

**BRITISH/CANADIAN FORCES, AT THE
COMMENCEMENT OF THE BATTLE OF FORT
GEORGE, MAY 27, 1813[*4]**

8th (King's) Regiment (Major Ogilvie), 310 other
ranks
Royal Newfoundland Regiment (Captain Winters),
40 other ranks
Glengarry Light Infantry Regiment (Captain Liddell,
Captain Roxburgh), 90 other ranks
Captain Runchey's Company of Colour (Captain
Runchey), 27 other ranks
2nd Lincoln Militia Regiment (Colonel Nichol), 100
other ranks
Native Warriors (Captain Norton), 20 warriors

Winfield Scott. This officer had been previously captured at Queenston Heights and then allowed to return to the U.S. after having sworn a parole not to engage in any military action until officially exchanged, and was, therefore, in the official opinion of Sir George Prevost and the British government, blatantly breaking his word of honour and parole, as no *mutually* agreed exchange had taken place.

Library and Archives Canada, C-23675.

The Invasion at Fort George. This published image was copied from an eye-witness pencil sketch made by surgeon A. Trowbridge while he was serving with the American fleet. Fort Niagara is the flagged fortification on the left bank of the river. Fort George, the flagged fortification on the right bank. The town of Newark and Mississauga Point Lighthouse (centre). The British Two Mile Creek battery (flagged small fortification at right), toward which the American vanguard of boats are pulling. The huge cloud of white "smoke" behind the main forts is actually spray from the Great Falls, clearly visible, over twelve miles (20 kilometers) away.

On shore, although General Vincent ordered an immediate redeployment toward the lakefront, the first defenders destined to face the Americans were detachments from the Glengarry Light Infantry, the Royal Newfoundland Regiment, Runchey's Coloured Corps, the Lincoln Militia, and a party of Norton's Native warriors, totalling no more than 300 men.[4] However, despite being stationed directly in front of the approaching enemy, they could not immediately engage them, as cannon fire from the American fleet scoured the elevated open ground overlooking the landing beach. As a result, they

From the Conger Goodyear Manuscript Collection, Volume 9, Courtesy of the Buffalo and Erie County Historical Society Research Library, Buffalo, NY.

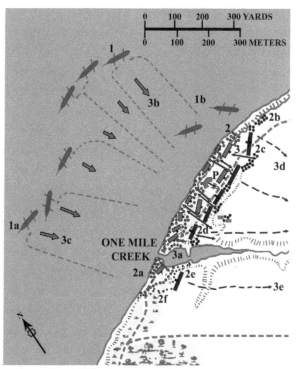

Lieutenant Colonel Winfield Scott, commander of the initial wave of invading American troops. By leading this attack he was, according to the British, in flagrant breach of his parole, given at the time of his capture at Queenston the previous October.

THE BATTLE OF FORT GEORGE, THE FIGHT FOR THE LANDING GROUND (8:00–9:00 a.m.)

P   Detached gun battery at One Mile Creek

1. The main American flotilla (1, 1a) takes up station opposite One Mile Creek to cover the amphibious landing, while other vessels move inshore (1b) and bombard the covering shore battery (P).

2. U.S. advance forces (2, 2a) land under fire from a composite force of British regulars, Canadian militia (2b, 2c, 2d, 2e), and Native allies (2f), and are initially contained on the beach.

3. U.S. forces (3, 3a) make a number of unsuccessful attempts to push off the beach, resulting in a succession of close-quarter engagements that fluctuate across the open ground above the landing ground. With the landing of an increasing number of American troops (3b, 3c), supported by artillery fire from the fleet, the defenders suffer enough casualties that they are forced to retire to a new position away from the waterfront (3d, 3e).

were forced to take cover under the lee of a nearby small ravine, while the crew of the solitary artillery battery positioned above the landing ground were also soon forced to abandon their position for cover.

As the American boats moved further inshore, they masked (blocked the firing of) the naval guns, allowing the small force of defenders to advance and fire into the packed boats as they pressed toward the shoreline. Once the Americans began to land, however, the defenders positions on the higher ground made them prominent targets and they began to suffer casualties accordingly. Falling back, they were quickly followed by American troops, who scaled the sandy escarpment fronting the beach and engaged the composite defensive units in a severe firefight and hand-to-hand combat. Eventually, the Americans were driven back to the beach, from which they continued firing at the once-again-exposed British troops. For a second time, the British retired and Americans pressed forward, culminating in another cycle of hand-to-hand combat, the Americans withdrawing to the beach to await yet more reinforcements and the renewed deadly fire of the American naval artillery curtailing the temporary victory by the defenders. With the backing of additional American troops from General Boyd's brigade, Winfield Scott led his men onto the upper ground for the third time, only to find the surviving defenders had retired about 200 yards (183 meters)

THE AMERICANS OVERWHELM THE INITIAL DEFENDER'S POSITIONS (9:00–10:30 a.m.)

O   Lighthouse gun battery
P   Detached gun battery at One Mile Creek

1. British forces retreating from the beach (1, 1a) are reinforced (1b) and establish a new line-of-battle (1c, 1d).

2. A composite British force (2, 2a), moves up from Fort George to establish a defensive position near to the Presbyterian church (2b, 2c), but far enough away from the waterfront to avoid gunfire from elements of the American flotilla that are moving up into the river mouth (2d).

3. Backed by additional waves of reinforcements (3, 3a), U.S. forces move off the beach and advance on the British line (3b, 3c). While heavy, close-quarter firing results in significant casualties on both sides, overwhelming American firepower decimates the British line. Consequently, the British break off and begin to retreat (3d, 3e).

4. Remnants of the beachhead British force (4, 4a) retreat through the woods and gully of One Mile Creek. Reaching the secondary British position, some of these units reform on the left flank of the British force (4b, 4c), while others leave the area or retreat to Fort George (4d).

and had also been reinforced by a detachment of around 300 men of the 8th (King's) Regiment. On the British side, Colonel Myers had assembled a force around 570 men, while General Boyd's brigade of troops augmented Scott's force to create an attacking strength of over 2,300 infantry. After

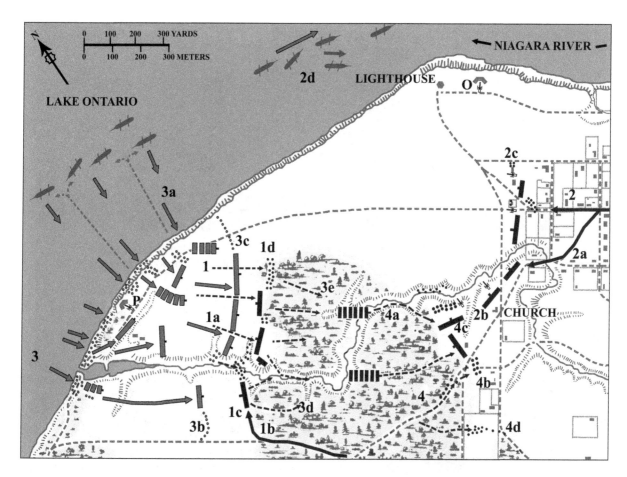

advancing toward the British troops, the opposing lines blazed away at each other, sometimes at a range of less than fifteen yards (13 meters) apart.

Inevitably, the overwhelmingly superior firepower of the American combined force tore apart the British line, killing or wounding almost every field officer. After suffering over 300 casualties, the British began to give way and retired toward the town by way of the wooded gully of One Mile Creek. Farther back, Lieutenant Colonel Harvey had been able to move up a composite force of several companies of the 49th Regiment, two of Incorporated Militia, and

Looking east along the Lake Ontario shoreline toward the location of the American landing. Note the high embankment, which the invading Americans had to scale to engage the British forces on the open ground above.

The Presbyterian church at Newark, the site of heavy fighting during the May 27 battle. The church was burned down by the Americans later that summer.

THE MAIN ENGAGEMENT TAKES PLACE NEAR THE PRESBYTERIAN CHURCH IN NEWARK (10:30–11:30 a.m.)

O   Lighthouse gun battery
P   Detached gun battery at One Mile Creek

1. After seeing the British disengage and retire, the main American force (1) forms into columns and waits for additional reinforcements (1a). They then advance along the shoreline in two main columns (1b, 1c), protected on the right by their light troops in the woods (1d) and their fleet on the left (1e).

2. Approaching the lighthouse at Mississauga Point, the U.S. columns (2) are confronted by the British Force on their flank (2a, 2b). In response, the Americans wheel into line and engage (2c, 2d), backed by gunfire from the American flotilla (2e).

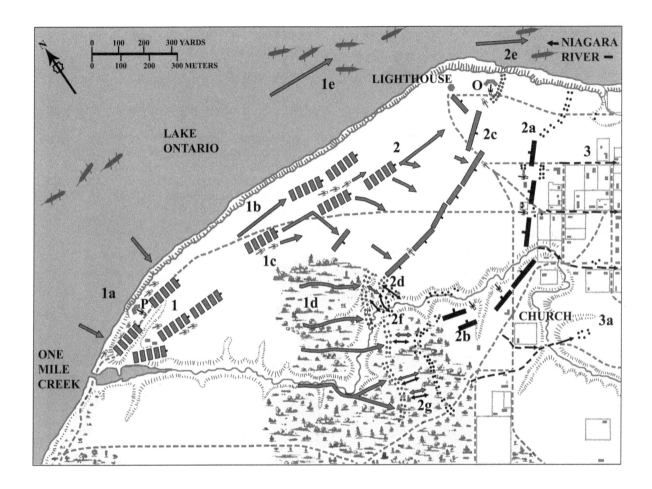

At the same time, the U.S. light troops advancing through the woods on the American right flank are engaged by reformed British and Canadian units in a close-quarter fight that subsequently ebbs and flows through the dense woods (2f, 2g).

3. Following fierce fighting and after suffering additional heavy losses, depleted British and Canadian units (3, 3a) begin to retreat toward Fort George, spiking and abandoning the riverside batteries as they go.

his ad hoc units of Embodied Militia volunteers and invalids, backed by every available artillery crew and their field guns. These troops, supplemented as time passed by detachments retreating from the beachhead fight, now took up a new position in front of the town, near the Presbyterian church, and awaited the appearance of the enemy.

Back at the landing zone, the Americans did not follow the retreating British through the woods. Instead, they formed into three columns and advanced across the open ground, paralleling the shoreline, thus ensuring that they remained under the cover of the guns aboard their fleet. On the right, Winfield Scott's column included detachments that infiltrated the woods, securing that flank and probing ahead, trying to outflank the British left flank. In the centre was Boyd's main infantry force of the Sixth, Fifteenth, and part of the Sixteenth Regiments, supported by four artillery pieces; while on the left, nearest the waterfront, were the remainder of the Sixteenth Regiment with four more artillery pieces. Since no limber horses had accompanied the artillery on shore, moving the guns and limbers was done by "volunteers" from the infantry and the gun crews, who manhandled the heavy equipment over the uneven ground. Despite facing this overwhelming number of troops, Harvey's line opened fire on the approaching American columns and, despite taking significant casualties, held back the repeated

THE BRITISH RETREAT FROM FORT GEORGE AND NEWARK (11:30 a.m.–1:00 p.m.)

H, L, M, N   British detached riverside gun batteries

I, J, K   British battery positions at Fort George

1. Depleted British units (1, 1a) retreat through Newark, and attempt to reform behind Fort George (1b). However, Chauncey's flotilla (1c) outflanks the exposed British right flank, forcing a general evacuation from all the remaining British battery positions (1d), Fort George, and Butler's Barracks.

2. Remaining elements of the militias and Native allies at Butler's Barracks march to join in the retreat toward Queenston (2).

3. Surviving British-Canadian and Native allied units begin a full-scale retreat toward Queenston (3), covered in part by detachments of Incorporated Militia (3a).

4. After seeing the British disengage and retire, Major General Lewis orders the main American force to wait until all American reinforcements have arrived before cautiously advancing on Fort George (4, 4a).

5. U.S. light forces and detachments of militia (5) press forward upon the American right flank to secure Butler's Barracks (5a), then advance on Fort George, but only capture some British wounded, stragglers, and women (5b).

6. Against orders, Winfield Scott commands his light troops to pursue the British (6, 6a).

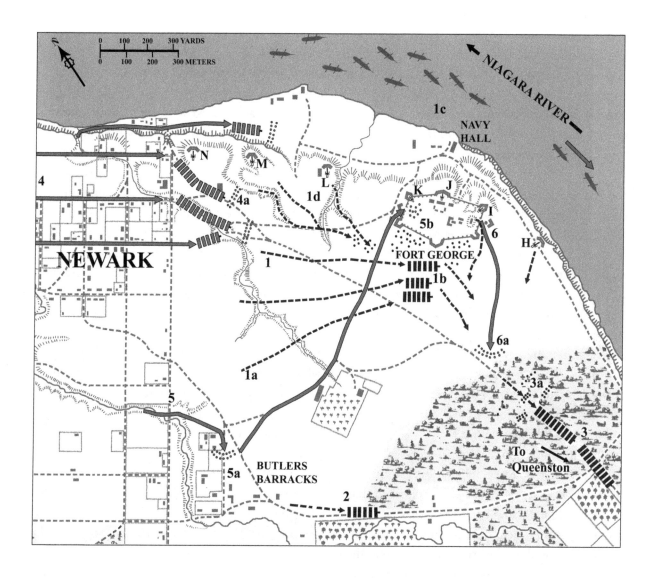

attacks of the American centre for over half an hour — and it should be noted that it was the guns of the British artillery that were particularly successful in stalling the enemy's advance. But once Scott's Light troops successfully outflanked the British left wing and the main line was in danger of being surrounded, Harvey was forced to order a retreat through the town to the garrison common, behind Fort George.

Seeing the British line moving away, several of the American senior officers prepared for a rapid advance, but were immediately curtailed by Major General Morgan Lewis, the senior officer in the field and effective commander of the army (as the ailing General Dearborn had chosen to remain onboard ship during the attack). Lewis was a savvy politician and former governor of New York State, but was an officer of virtually no battlefield experience and had the disasters of Hull, Van Rensselaer, and Smyth looming before him. Fearful of a trap, Lewis delayed for over an hour while the final landings augmented his force to over 4,000 men before ordering the advance continue.

By this time, Harvey and Vincent had rallied their depleted forces behind the burned-out remnants of Fort George and were prepared to make a last stand here. However, this decision was soon rendered moot when vessels from the American flotilla anchored in the river and brought their guns to bear upon the open ground both in front and behind the fort, thus cutting off any hope of making a stand in the open, or getting reinforcements from upriver. In addition, reports came in of American troop movements at Youngstown, threatening an American envelopment of the defenders from the rear. Fronted by a force vastly outnumbering his own, and threatened on his flanks and rear by potential movements of the enemy, Vincent ordered the evacuation of the ruined Fort George, the destruction of all supplies and ammunition that could not be carried off, and the spiking of all guns that could not be withdrawn. To the sounds of detonation, Vincent and his remaining troops retreated through the woods toward Queenston, while Norton's Native warriors and a detachment of Incorporated Militia provided the rearguard.

Brigadier General Vincent initially considered retiring to Fort Erie, where he hoped to dig-in while awaiting reinforcements from Proctor's force at Amherstburg. However, after being warned by Colonel Nichol and Lieutenant Colonel Harvey that this would effectively trap the British forces if the Americans pressed their victory, Vincent ordered the retreat be made to Beaver Dams instead, while orders were sent to Bisshopp's troops to destroy their posts and retire on Vincent's new position.[5]

Meanwhile, when the American force eventually emerged from the town and cautiously approached Fort George (fearing the explosions they heard

OFFICIAL CASUALTIES, BATTLE OF FORT GEORGE, MAY 27, 1813[5]

American

Advance, Light Troops, (Lieutenant Colonel Scott)
Killed: 23 other ranks
Wounded: 2 officers, 64 other ranks

1st Brigade (Brigadier General Boyd)
Killed: 1 officer, 87 other ranks
Wounded: 3 officers, 117 other ranks

2nd Brigade (Brigadier General Winder)
Wounded: 6 other ranks

3rd Brigade (Brigadier General Chandler)
No Casualties

British Regulars

Killed: 3 officers, 49 other ranks*
Wounded: 1 staff, 10 officers, 33 other ranks*
Missing: 1 officer, 8 drummers, 253 other ranks*

Canadian Militias

Killed and Wounded: 85 all ranks
Paroled: 507 all ranks (including local non-combatant men and boys rounded up after the battle)

Native Allies

Killed and Wounded: Unknown (at least 2)

*According to General Boyd's subsequent account, the British casualty figures were significantly higher: "We buried 107 of the enemy on the bank where the first stand was made; 105 prisoners were taken in the engagement; 175 wounded fell into our hands." Another American account gave the British casualty totals as:

Killed: 105 all ranks
Prisoners: Wounded: 4 officers, 159 other ranks
Unwounded: 3 officers, 110 other ranks Including 124 men left behind in hospital

would presage a detonation similar to that of York), they found the main force of defenders gone and the only prisoners that fell into their hands were the wounded, the sick, some wives and dependants of the soldiers, and a detachment that had delayed too long in their assignment of destroying anything that would prove useful to the enemy. They also found an unconscious Winfield Scott, who had pressed ahead of his own troops into the fort and been struck by debris from an exploding magazine. Fortunately for the American cause, his only injury was a broken collarbone, which did not slow the warrior down

Library and Archives Canada, C-040034.

Butler's Barracks, J.P. Cockburn, artist, 1829. A view of the road leading into Newark, with Butler's Barracks on the right and Fort Niagara visible in the distance (centre) beyond the Niagara River, detail from the larger painting. *Library and Archives Canada, C-040034.*

one jot. The first secure foothold in Upper Canada had been attained — the only problem was that the enemy was gone, so which direction should the victorious army march to do battle and rout the retreating foe? Colonel Scott was in little doubt of the direction taken by the British and "deemed it his duty to institute and continue a pursuit of five miles; not merely without orders, but in evasion of such as were given."[6] But he was soon frustrated by General Lewis, who feared a trap and counterattack within the dense woods surrounding the area and sent Scott an order "of a character so decided and peremptory as by leaving nothing to discretion, could

not fail to recall him to Fort George."[7]

Late that afternoon, Vincent's order to retire reached Lieutenant Colonel Bisshopp at Fort Erie and the evacuation of all regular troops and field guns was begun. Only a detachment of the 3rd Lincoln Militia was left behind to destroy the magazines and spike the heavier garrison artillery that could not be removed. Instead of fruitlessly disposing of this resource, however, Major John Warren and his detachment undertook to expend every pound of powder and shot by bombarding the enemy batteries on the opposite shore — a task they kept up for most of the night. Around dawn they set about destroying the remaining stores and for-tifications. Having accomplished this task, Warren officially dismissed his militiamen to either return to their homes, or retreat and join up with the militia units stationed along the Grand River. The Niagara frontier was now open for an American occupation. According to the official American history of that day, Fort Erie was "captured" by a detachment of the Twelfth Infantry Regiment (Lieutenant Colonel Preston). However, what is not in the official history is that prior to Preston's occupation, an American naval surgeon, Usher Parsons, had made his own entirely unofficial "capture" of the fort.

At 7 o'clock this morning the enemy blew up their magazines at the fort. In the afternoon Dr. Purcell and myself, with one citizen and about 20 others (sail-ors), seeing no Centinels on the opposite shore crossed over ... we were provided with a white handkerchief to wave if the enemy appeared.... We found no enemy and ventured to march towards Fort Erie not without some apprehensions of dan-ger. But we met no one until near the fort when two portly looking gentlemen came out with a flag of truce. I left the men with Dr. Purcell and went with the gentle-men.... They asked for protection of their private property ... but first desired me to calm the fears of the women who were assembled in a room and much fright-ened, which I did in a brief speech. I found an abundance of military stores, cloathing, arms, etc. and calling to my troops rigged them out with a full suit and then marched them back to the boat.... We returned to Black Rock and sent an anonymous note to the Col. at Buffalo that the enemy had left Fort Erie. I feared to send my name because I had violated all rules and disci-pline by my expedition. He embarked his regiment (first ascertaining that the Centinels were not to be seen) and crossed over in the evening and took possession of Fort Erie. I crossed over again in the even-ing and stayed all night.[8]

— *Diary of Usher Parsons*,
May 28, 1813

By the following day, the burned out British positions at Chippawa, Queenston, and Fort George were all being garrisoned by American troops. One immediate consequence of this loss of British con-trol of the upper reaches of the Niagara River was that the Americans were able to tow out five armed vessels from their navy yard on the Scajaquada

Creek and load them with vitally needed supplies for delivery to the shipbuilding yards at Erie, Pennsylvania, on Lake Erie, completely reversing the balance of naval power on that lake.

Despite having suffered severely in losses of manpower and supplies, most of Vincent's surviving troops, especially the militia and Native allies, expected that their commander would concentrate his forces at Beaver Dams and then make a counter-offensive on the American invaders, especially once the troops from Chippawa, Fort Erie, Burlington Heights, and additional parties of Native warriors from the Grand River were added to the sum. Instead, and to their grave concern, directives arrived for the commandeering of every wagon in the area and the destruction of any stores and supplies that could not be immediately transported, as the army was ordered to retreat to Forty Mile Creek.

This further withdrawal was ordered because Vincent had received disturbing reports of the Americans re-embarking a substantial number of troops on board their fleet with orders to sail along the lake and land behind his already diminished army, thus trapping it between two enemy divisions. It was therefore essential that he move quickly, before his options ran out. Despite this valid tactical necessity, many of the officers of the militia, as well as Norton and his Native warriors, took this action as proof that Vincent's intention was to completely abandon the Niagara to the Americans and possibly retire on York or even Kingston. Indeed, after remaining less than two days at the eminently defendable position at Forty Mile Creek, when new orders were issued that the army was to continue in its retreat to Burlington Heights their fear became a virtual certainty. Furthermore, far from being encouraged to stay with the regulars and continue to fight the invaders, most of the militia units were officially disbanded and told to return to their homes to await the advancing Americans and submit to certain capture and possible imprisonment or parole. As a result, morale plummeted, the Native warriors left en masse to see to the protection of their families and homes along the Grand River, and even the most ardent Crown supporters wondered if this was the end of Upper Canada as a province. Everything now hinged on the actions of the Americans.

CHAPTER 5

Victories, But for Whom?

Despite having achieved major military victories at Fort York and Fort George, instead of being lauded as the hero of the hour, Major General Dearborn found himself beset by the old adage that bad news often comes in threes.

First, according to his original plan, following the successful conclusion of his invasion of the Niagara frontier, Dearborn's army was to have moved west to link up with Major General Harrison's forces to recover the Michigan Territory. Unfortunately, this entire part of the campaign had been effectively scuttled by the unexpected aggressiveness of Brigadier General Proctor and his forces at Amherstburg.

Ever since the death of General Brock, in October 1812, General Proctor had been repeatedly denied more than a trickle of reinforcements and supplies by General Sheaffe, who favoured defending the Niagara frontier. In addition, Proctor's latest intelligence reports indicated that the balance of power in the west had swung dramatically in favour of the Americans. There were three reasons for this:

- The loss of York in April had included the town's warehouses, which contained vital naval construction materials destined for the shipyard at Amherstburg. Those supplies had either been burned or fallen into the hands of the Americans.
- The British abandonment of Fort Erie had allowed the previously trapped American vessels at Black Rock to escape and unite with the new ships being constructed at the Americans' Lake Erie Naval Base at Erie (PA).
- A new set of massive fortifications (Fort Meigs) was being constructed on the Maumee River,

and would almost certainly become Harrison's base of operations for a new campaign to retake the Michigan Territory and possibly invade Upper Canada.

While Proctor knew there was nothing he could do about the events at York and Erie, the more time Harrison had to complete his preparations the more dangerous and difficult it would be for Proctor's diminished and poorly supplied forces to eliminate this base or stop any subsequent invasion. Believing that he had no realistic alternative, and despite the considerable odds against it succeeding, Proctor ordered a pre-emptive offensive operation to besiege and capture Fort Meigs. For this campaign he cobbled together a combined force of 533 British regulars, 63 Fencibles, 462 Canadian militia, and 1,200 Native warriors.[1]

THE SIEGE OF FORT MEIGS, MAY 1–9, 1813

Sailing from Amherstburg on April 23rd, Proctor's force landed at the mouth of the Maumee River that evening. They then had to overcome bad weather and mud choked trackways as they hauled their cannon overland, eventually reaching Fort Meigs on April 29th, whereupon they began erecting siege lines. By May 1st artillery batteries were erected on both the north and south sides of the Maumee River and they began a bombardment of the fort from two flanks. Following four days of round-the-clock firing, and constantly being berated by his Native allies for engaging in a siege rather than making an immediate frontal attack, Proctor still did not think that enough damage had been done to make any formal assault practicable.

Inside the fort, however, General Harrison was deeply concerned about his defensive capabilities. The British artillery barrage was inflicting such a degree of damage on his fortifications that it required constant repairs to maintain the defences. In addition, casualties had mounted to the point where he had been forced to build numerous earth embankments within the fort to shelter his troops from the artillery fire. Finally, his own lack of artillery ammunition required him to issue an offer of payment for each spent British cannonball that was located and brought in for reuse by the American batteries. Thus, when he received word on May 4th that a relief column of 1,200 Kentucky militia were approaching his position, Harrison decided to make an attempt to break the siege. He therefore communicated his plan to the commander of the relief column, Brigadier General Green Clay, for the two forces to work in concert. The following morning, forces from Fort Meigs made a sortie to attack the southern British batteries from the front. At the same time, the relief force moved forward in two columns. The "northern" column, under Colonel William Dudley, consisted of some 800 men in twelve boats. Their orders were to sail up the river and land on the northern bank of the Maumee River, destroy the northern British artillery positions, and then withdraw to the fort. Simultaneously, the "southern" column of 400 men, under General Clay in six boats, was to fight its way overland directly toward the southern batteries, catching the enemy between itself and Harrison's sortie.

Initially, the American plan met with some success, with the northern battery being overrun and the guns spiked. However, a portion of the Kentucky militia disobeyed their explicit orders to maintain regimental discipline and went on a rampaging chase of Proctor's retreating Native allies. In the thick forest the Natives ambushed the incautious militiamen, inflicting a catastrophic number of casualties. At the same time, a strong counterattack by the Essex and Kent Embodied Militias, backed by men of the 41st Regiment, soon recaptured the batteries and routed those Kentuckians who had obeyed Harrison's orders. By the time the fighting ended, of the 800 men originally in this northern American force only 150 are recorded as escaping back to their boats. At the same time, the sortie from the fort also initially succeeded in penetrating the British lines and spiking some of the guns before they too were

evicted by a counterattack. Clay's southern column came under heavy fire while in the process of landing, and instead of attacking the British positions, took only what they could carry, abandoned their boats, and diverted directly to the fort. They linked up with Harrison's garrison, but lost the remainder of their supplies and boats as plunder to the British and Native warriors.

Despite suffering heavy losses, which the Americans only officially listed as 81 killed and 189 wounded, Harrison's garrison had gained some of the extra manpower and supplies it desperately needed and was able to continue to hold out. Proctor's army, despite having recovered his batteries and inflicted such severe casualties on the enemy (having taken some thirty-four American officers and 420 other ranks prisoner alone), had also suffered a significant number of casualties during the attack (killed: 14 other ranks; wounded: 2 officers, 46 other ranks; prisoner: 2 officers, 39 other ranks).

By the end of the week, General Proctor was faced with the unpleasant fact that he could no longer maintain his siege and would have to retreat back to Amherstburg. This seemingly surprising turn of events came about quite simply — the majority of Proctor's Native and militia troops had deserted from the siege lines. This was partially because, having already become encumbered by large amounts of booty and trophies of war, the Natives became angry and considered themselves betrayed by the British when they were denied what they considered their right to collect further trophies or exact reprisals upon captured American prisoners, as was their custom. This situation became critical when, witnessing a group of Natives starting to rob and then attack a group of unarmed American prisoners, British soldiers had stepped in to halt the potential massacre. When this had proved useless, as the Native depredations continued, the British troops were left with no choice but to fight off their own supposed allies, at the cost of several men wounded and at least one killed from their own ranks. This serious incident fatally fractured the alliance and caused all but a handful of warriors to abandon the siege. In the case of the militia, the campaign had been started at the crucial point of the season when the men were most needed at home to plant their crops. As a result, following the submission of a strongly worded petition outlining their desperate concerns, many of the militiamen decided that their personal need to return to their homesteads for crop planting had become a higher priority (to prevent the future starvation of their families), than maintaining a drawn-out encirclement of an enemy fort in the middle of nowhere.

Nonetheless, even with the eventual withdrawal of Proctor's forces on May 9th, the combined effect of the American losses at the battle of Fort Meigs, the damage to the fort, and the substantial negative impact it had on subsequent American efforts to recruit a new militia force, especially in Kentucky, meant that the campaign to retake Michigan and invade Upper Canada through the Detroit corridor was crippled for the foreseeable future. Consequently, General Dearborn and his army on the Niagara was the sole thrust of American operations against the enemy in Upper Canada.

Second in Dearborn's list of troubles was that the general's own command was beset by discontent and dissent. Always a temperamental commander, General Dearborn had increasingly favoured a clique of handpicked subordinates and isolated himself from his other officers. Now in failing health, and increasingly "crusty" in temper, his daily command duties had been assumed by an "outsider," his ambitious second-in-command, Major General Morgan Lewis. This officer was one who Dearborn had previously dismissed as "totally destitute of any practical qualifications necessary for an officer of his rank."[2]. In return, Lewis was no less contemptuous of "Granny" Dearborn and, seeing the victory at Fort George as his own, resented Dearborn garnering any credit for the action. Under this mutual antipathy, Lewis therefore saw no dereliction of his duty in detailing Dearborn's command shortcomings within private reports to his brother-in-law, the secretary of war, John Armstrong. In addition,

Lewis had his own set of supporters, which created a level of vicious political infighting within the American regimental commands that far outstripped Hull's similar situation the previous year at Detroit. Consequently, following the battle at Fort George, when criticism arose over the failure of the entire American force to aggressively pursue the British forces in its retreat to Queenston and the recall of Winfield Scott from his advanced position, Lewis wasted no time in falsely claiming the order came directly from Dearborn, an assertion Dearborn vehemently denied.

In response to these allegations of lethargy, Dearborn ordered Lewis to march out with almost half the army in pursuit of the retreating Crown forces, but did not stipulate any specific destination. Lewis, however, was not prepared to march off into the unknown and demanded that he be given, in writing, a more explicit set of orders. Dearborn responded by directing Lewis to move on Queenston and then advance to Beaver Dams. Lewis, on the other hand, believed that the British had already left Beaver Dams and were heading toward Forty Mile Creek. He therefore contradicted his commanding officer and demanded to have his route changed so that he could cut off Vincent's retreat, or at least catch and attack him while Vincent was on the march and unable to prepare any proper defences. He also pressed for a simultaneous naval

landing of troops at Head-of-the-Lake (Hamilton) to ensure Vincent's encirclement.

Retorting that Lewis' information was a deliberate ploy by Vincent to send the Americans in the wrong direction, Dearborn categorically ordered Lewis to follow his previously assigned route. However, later, after Lewis had marched for Queenston, Dearborn had second thoughts and authorized the preparation of some of the remaining units for transportation up the lake if further intelligence revealed the British were on the march. A fact soon conveyed to Vincent (who *was* still at Beaver Dams) and actually precipitated his further retreat — which in turn prevented Lewis' troops from intercepting him.

Reaching Queenston Heights, Lewis' troops found only the debris of Vincent's retreat, while the enemy continued to elude them. Because of poor logistical support, Lewis' column had marched without securing a sufficiency of provisions or camp equipment. Consequently they were hungry, footsore, tired, and soaked (as intermittent downpours of rain drenched them). Sending out foraging parties to appropriate all available food, Lewis' troops occupied any building that offered shelter from the inclement weather and settled down for the night. At the same time, back at Fort George, Dearborn received confirmed reports of Vincent's retreat. In response, instead of directing Lewis to march directly toward the enemy and sending him additional support, Dearborn sent him written orders to detach General Chandler's brigade back to the fort as quickly as possible. Reluctantly complying with his commander's demands the following morning, Lewis was still determined to initiate his own pursuit with what remained of his force and ordered an immediate advance, only to receive yet another set of written orders from Dearborn. These specifically terminated Lewis' plans, reducing him to providing garrison forces at Queenston, Chippawa, and Fort Erie, and then returning to Fort George with the rump remnant of his detached command. Furious and frustrated at being thwarted yet again, Lewis had, ironically, been hoist on his own petard — as his earlier demands for more specific written orders from Dearborn came back with a vengeance to curtail his independence of command.

Reaching Burlington Heights on the evening of May 31st, Brigadier General Vincent and his troops had immediately begun to dig-in. Outnumbered by at least three to one, Vincent knew that, barring a miracle, he had a vital decision to make as to his further movements. His position at Burlington Heights allowed him to continue to supply Brigadier General Proctor and the Lake Erie fleet. Any further retreat would cut that lifeline and effectively hand the western end of Upper Canada to the Americans. On the other hand, Vincent also recognized that if he remained in position, the Americans could use their naval superiority to recross Lake Ontario, land troops in his rear, and cut off his own retreat to York and Kingston. Fortunately, the Americans remained at Fort George, which persuaded Vincent to hold his position and send urgent appeals to Prevost at Kingston to send up reinforcements and supplies aboard Sir James Yeo's flotilla. In the meantime, Embodied Militia volunteers, three companies of the Incorporated Militia, and bands of Native warriors secured the flanks of the British position, reported on American movements, and collected any supplies of food and abandoned equipment that could be found along the line of the retreat, thus denying them to the enemy.

Unbeknownst to General Vincent, his earlier appeals for reinforcements and supplies and the latest news of the American inertia at the mouth of the Niagara had another effect entirely when they were received at Kingston by Sir James Yeo and Sir George Prevost. For although it had been their original intention to support Vincent before the Americans took Fort George, this new development was seen as a heaven-sent opportunity to destroy Sackets Harbor, the base of Chauncey's naval power on Lake Ontario, and simultaneously cut the American main supply line to the Niagara, thus creating the third circumstance that was to bedevil General Dearborn.

Sir James Yeo, overall commander of the British and colonial Naval forces in Upper Canada.

THE BATTLE OF SACKETS HARBOR, MAY 29, 1813

Following the American victory at York, activities at Sackets Harbor had been closely monitored and reported on by Prevost's agents, who sent detailed intelligence on the continued build up of troops at the harbour. As a result, when Chauncey and his fleet returned on May 11th, the state of alert at Kingston was raised by that same evening. On May 26th, Sir George Prevost recorded his observations in a report to Earl Bathurst about the current situation:

> The enemy, continuing to avail themselves of their naval ascendancy on Lake Ontario, left Sacketts Harbour on the 20th inst. & have appeared off Fort George with sixteen vessels laden with troops, which they disembarked the following day.... Col. Vincent being apprehensive of an immediate attack from a force in number vastly superior to his own, I have advised Commodore Sir J's Yeo to sail with the vessels ready for service to reconnoitre the enemy's flotilla, in order that he may form an opinion upon the practicability of conveying about three hundred men, being the whole disposable force I can command at present and which are held in readiness to embark at a moments notice ...[3]

Prevost also directed Yeo to make a reconnaissance toward Sackets Harbor, to confirm the absence of any interception threat from Chauncey's fleet if Yeo's flotilla sailed with Vincent's reinforcements. At noon the following day, Yeo returned post-haste to Kingston, bearing news that the enemy's principal

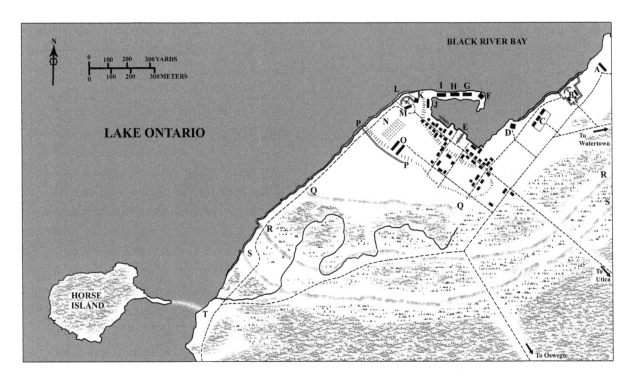

shipbuilding centre was indeed empty of shipping. With the combined reports from Vincent and Chauncey, and looking to take advantage of the moment, Prevost decided to completely revise his campaign strategy and make an immediate surprise strike at Sackets Harbor, before Chauncey's fleet could return. Without any proper preparations of supply, artillery support, ammunition, food, or even a coherent plan of action, during the course of the afternoon of May 27th every available vessel was assembled and loaded with detachments of troops.[*4]

By evening the ad hoc attack force of some 900 men was embarked and the flotilla sailed south to attack Sackets Harbor. Awaiting them was a composite American garrison force that was, according to various sources, comprised of between 1,450 to nearly 2,000 men, drawn from units of regular and militia infantry, artillery, naval crews, U.S. Marines, dockyard workers, and local volunteers.

At dawn the following day, while still some miles from their target and under light intermittent winds, the British flotilla was sighted by a

SACKETS HARBOR AND ITS DEFENSIVE POSITIONS, MAY 1813

A   Hospital
B   Fort Volunteer with artillery position
C   Barracks
D   Blockhouse
E   Naval dockyard (with the future *General Pike* under construction on the stocks, and the *Duke of Gloucester*, previously captured at York, at the quayside)
F   Navy Point, Blockhouse
G   Navy Point, Lower Artillery Battery/ Barracks/Storehouse
H   Navy Point, Middle Artillery Battery/ Barracks/Storehouse
I   Navy Point, Upper Artillery Battery/ Barracks/Storehouse
J   Warehouse
K   Fort Tompkins, Blockhouse
L   Fort Tompkins Artillery Battery (32-pounder)
M   Fort Tompkins, Marine Barracks
N   Tented encampment
O   Basswood Cantonment Barracks
P   Drainage ditch
Q   Inner line of abattis (*constructed late spring 1813)
R   Middle line of abattis (*constructed February 1813, incomplete and overgrown)
S   Outer line of abattis (*constructed February 1813, incomplete and overgrown)
T   Mainland end of the partially submerged sandbar connecting to Horse Island

BATTLE OF SACKETS HARBOR, MAY 29, 1813[14]

British

Fleet
Moria
Beresford
Sir Sidney Smith
Wolfe
Royal George
(estimated 35 gunboats, open boats, and bateaux)

Landing Force
1st (Royal Scots) Regiment (not specified), est. 30 all ranks
8th (King's) Regiment (Colonel Robert Young/ Major Thomas Evans), est. 200 all ranks
100th Regiment (Grenadier Company), est. 60 all ranks
104th Regiment (Major William Drummond), est. 350 all ranks
Royal Newfoundland Regiment (Not Specified), est. 100 all ranks
Glengarry Light Infantry Regiment (Captain McPherson), est. 50 all ranks
Royal Artillery (2 x 6-pounders and crews), est. 35 all ranks
Lower Canada Canadian Voltigeur Regiment (Major Frederick H. Heriot), 140 all ranks
Native Allies (Lieutenant Bernard St. Germain), 37 Mississauga and Mohawk warriors

Library and Archives Canada, C-8153.

(Above) *South East View of Sackett's Harbour*, copied from the original engraving by W.Strickland, 1815. (Below) The same viewpoint in 2012.

line of three American picket boats left behind by Chauncey for exactly this situation. Swinging about, the *Lady of the Lake* sailed westward toward the Niagara River to warn Chauncey, while the *Fair American* and *Pert* ran south, toward the American base, firing their cannons as an alarm warning. The element of surprise was now lost. In response, without any direct orders for a plan of attack and

seeking to maintain the initiative, Major William Drummond (104th) began to independently disembark some of his troops into his landing boats, intending to march overland to initiate the assault. However, in this he was abruptly overruled by Prevost, who ordered the troops re-embarkation and the continuation of the flotillas slow advance toward Sackets Harbor.

By later that morning, the wind had reversed direction and was blowing directly against the flotilla, causing it to lose way. With no hope of making a surprise attack, Prevost called off the landing and ordered the return of the expedition to Kingston. Almost immediately thereafter, however, the winds shifted once again and then subsided, becalming the fleet. At the same time, masthead lookouts reported the approach of a flotilla of eight large bateaux, rowing up from the south and obviously heading for the American harbour with what later was determined to be around 300 men from the Ninth and Twenty-First Regiments under Major Thomas Aspinwall's command at Oswego. To counter this reinforcement, a gunboat, manned by a detachment from the Glengarry Light Infantry, along with three large canoes filled with Native warriors, were ordered to engage the enemy and, if possible, force them to retreat. Coming under fire from the approaching British boats, far from engaging the smaller enemy units, or retiring as an intact unit, the American boats veered off and scattered, with the majority deliberately running themselves aground on the nearby lakeside shoreline. Whereupon the American troops aboard abandoned their vessels and made for the nearby woods at high speed. Following close behind, the Natives landed and chased after the fleeing Americans. In a series of hand-to-hand engagements in the woods, the

Americans were at a serious disadvantage and suffered casualties accordingly, losing over thirty-five men killed to the Natives' one. In fact, despite their numerical superiority, a large number of American troops were soon seen returning to their fully loaded bateaux, whereupon the boats set course directly for the becalmed British flotilla under a white flag. Upon their arrival, the some 115 troops aboard demanded British protection from the Natives as surrendered prisoners of war.

Despite being pleased by the turn out of events with the convoy, Prevost had nonetheless lost three hours in which to make his assault with favourable winds and his plan for a rapid strike was completely frustrated as the winds died and daylight ended. Faced with the choice of retiring to Kingston without being able to claim to have made any attempt to eliminate what others would consider a vulnerable American base, or attacking what he knew would now be a fully alerted and prepared enemy position, the deliberate surrender of Aspinwall's troops tipped the balance. Consequently, Prevost reversed his position yet again and ordered the attack to commence at first light the following morning.

On shore, the titular commander of the American base, Lieutenant Colonel Electus Backus (First Light Dragoons), had been making rushed preparations for the British assault from the moment the first alarm was raised. However, despite being

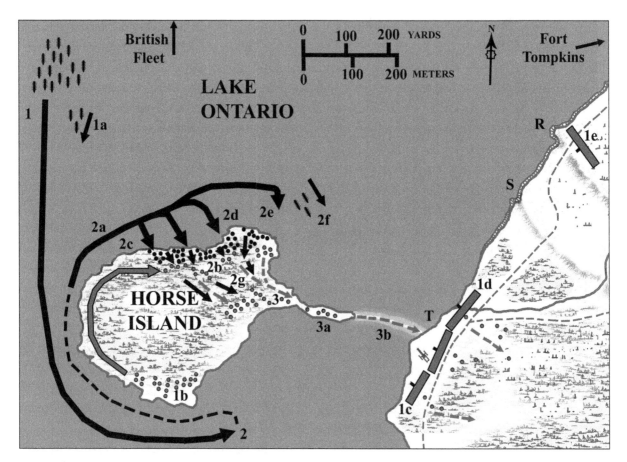

THE BRITISH LAND AT HORSE ISLAND (3:30–5:00 a.m.)

R   Middle line of abattis (*constructed February 1813, incomplete and overgrown)
S   Outer line of abattis (*constructed February 1813, incomplete and overgrown)
T   Mainland end of the partially submerged sandbar connecting to Horse Island

1. Because the main British fleet is becalmed offshore (off map), the landing boats (1) are forced to make their approach unsupported, except by a number of small gunboats (1a). Attempting to make their landing to the south of Horse Island, the flotilla comes under fire from the detachment of New York militia (Albany Republican Volunteers) stationed on the island (1b). In

addition, the intended landing ground is occupied and defended by a strong force of American militia (Fifty-Fifth and Seventy-Fifth regiments, plus unspecified detachments) (1c, 1d), supported by additional troops in reserve (detachments from the Ninth, Twenty-First, and Twenty-Third regiments) at the middle defensive abattis line (R, 1e).

2. Unable to make their intended landing, the British flotilla reverses course and sails round to the northern side of Horse Island (2, 2a) where they come under long-range fire from Fort Tompkins (off map) and the Albany Volunteers, who have also moved round the island (2b). Under a heavy fire from the American militia, the lead boats make landings at various points along the shoreline (2c, 2d) while the following boats (2e) move farther round the island to cut off the American defenders. The gunboats (2f) also open fire on the unseen enemy in the woods. Once on shore, the leading British formations push forward through dense bush, forcing the Americans to make a fighting withdrawal (2g).

3. Heavily outnumbered, the Albany Volunteers make a rapid withdrawal (3, 3a) across the partially submerged causeway (3b, T), to the main line of militia on the mainland (1c, 1d).

a regular army officer, he found himself increasingly superseded by the local militia commander, Brigadier General Jacob Brown. Brown had originally been directed by General Dearborn to only gather a reserve of 300 to 400 militia, in order to "aid" Backus and his official "regular" garrison in case of an attack. Instead, Brown reinterpreted this directive as an authorization and a direct request to take over command of Sackets Harbor and oversee its entire defence.

With the British fleet becalmed offshore as night fell, Brown implemented the defensive plan for the harbour created by Colonel Alexander Macomb in February and took it upon himself to personally direct the placement of each newly arriving detachment of militia troops and make plans for a fighting retreat to the holdout position of Fort Volunteer if the remainder of the positions fell. He also issued directives for all additional local militia units in the immediate region to march to the harbour to bolster the defensive forces. By the early hours of the morning all of the available American forces had been positioned.[*5]

Because much of the immediate coast was composed of sheer rock outcrops and low cliffs, the closest reasonable landing ground not covered by the defensive fortifications and artillery positions were to the south of the harbour at Horse Island. Offshore, the boats had been filled with troops since shortly after 10:00 p.m., awaiting the first light of dawn to begin their approach. As a result, despite the virtually calm wind conditions, a constant cold drizzle and onshore swell had given the exposed troops in the heavily packed small boats an uncomfortable and rocky night, while the local currents scattered the boats from their assigned stations.

**AMERICAN DISPOSITIONS,
BATTLE OF SACKETS HARBOR, MAY 29, 1813**[5]

**Lieutenant Colonel Electus Backus
(First U.S. Light Dragoons)**

Horse Island:
Albany Republican Volunteers (Lieutenant Colonel John Mills), 175 all ranks, plus 1 x 6-pounder and crew

Causeway waterside earthworks and emplacements:
Detachments of Fifty-Fifth and Seventy-Fifth Regiments of New York State Militia (Brigadier General James Brown, Lieutenant Colonel Anthony Sprague, Lieutenant Colonel Gersholm Tuttle), plus additional unidentified detachments from at least three other militia units. Combined estimate: 600 all ranks, plus 1 x 6-pounder and crew

First Line:
Detachments from the Ninth/Twenty-First/Twenty-Third U.S. Infantry Regiments (Colonel Electus Backus), est. 200 all ranks, plus 1 x 6-pounder and crew (Lieutenant Louis Laval)

Second Line:
First U.S. Light Dragoons (unmounted, acting as infantry) (Captain Thomas Helms and Captain Silas Halsey), est. 350 all ranks

Basswood Cantonment (Reserve):
Mounted Dragoons (Major Nelson Luckett, Captain A.P. Hayne), est. 100 all ranks

Fort Tompkins:
First U.S. Light Artillery (Lieutenant. Thomas Ketchum) 1 x 32-pounder, plus up to nineteen additional artillery pieces and crews, est. 45–200 all ranks

Fort Volunteer:
Third Artillery (Major Samuel Nye), est. 100 all ranks

Navy Point Batteries:
Lower: 1 x 32-pounder, 1 x 12-pounder, and crews
Middle: 2 x 6-pounders and crews
Upper: 1 x 18-pounder, 1 x 12-pounder, and crews
Plus dockyard workers, U.S. Navy, U.S. Marines (Lieutenant John Drury), est. 200 men

Total estimated, approximately 1,450–2,000 all ranks

Once it was light enough to see, the boat crews had the double effort of regaining their stations against the currents and starting the attack on time.

Looking to make their initial landing almost exactly where Brown had predicted, on the mainland to the south side of Horse Island, the British boats soon came under a heavy fire from both the detachments placed on the island, and the militia units on the mainland. Seeing their planned landing ground occupied by the enemy and taking increasing numbers of casualties, the flotilla veered off toward the north side of the island, only to expose themselves to the additional artillery fire of the 32-pounder gun placed at Fort Tompkins atop the bluffs overlooking the harbour. What they did not know was that even this approach had been sufficient to persuade some of Brown's militiamen to begin deserting.

Continuing to suffer casualties, the leading wave of boats landed on Horse Island, persuading the small detachment of American defenders to retire across the narrow and partially submerged causeway that linked the island to Brown's prepared entrenchments. Here they joined his remaining force of militia, apparently fully prepared to take on the British from an excellent defensive position. As far as Brown was concerned he had the British penned on an island, with only a single narrow route through which they could approach his prepared earthwork defences, manned with infantry and backed by artillery — everything that a defending commander could wish for to inflict the heaviest casualties on his enemy.

A current (2012) view of Horse Island, as seen from the positions taken by General Brown's militia forces at the start of the battle. The line of projections in the water that mark the partially submerged remnants of the sandbar causeway are indicated for clarity.

According to General Brown's later account of the action:

> Every exertion was then made [by myself] to inspire my little force with confidence, and assure them that if they would but lay firm and restrain their fire, I was confident that every man must nearly kill his man. I then took my position in the centre by the left of the men at the 6-pounder, directly in front of the column approaching from the island and all was silent with me....[6]

Unfortunately for Brown, the calibre of the men he was facing was that of regular troops, trained for battle and ready to take casualties to achieve their objective. Despite facing the prospect of advancing across an entirely exposed and partially submerged narrow causeway of shingle, sand, and soft mud some 300 yards (275 meters) long and at points less than ten feet (3 meters) wide, before reaching Brown's prepared entrenchments, the men of the 100th Regiment formed a narrow solid column and, after fixing bayonets and "porting arms," commenced a disciplined advance across the causeway that steadily increased in pace and culminated in a charging of the bayonets at the last moment. Faced with

THE AMERICAN MILITIA IS ROUTED AND THE BRITISH ADVANCE/PURSUIT BEGINS (5:00–6:30 a.m.)

Q   Inner line of abattis (*constructed late spring 1813)
R   Middle line of abattis (*constructed February 1813, incomplete and overgrown)
S   Outer line of abattis (*constructed February 1813, incomplete and overgrown)
T   Mainland end of the partially submerged sandbar connecting to Horse Island

1. Although under fire from Fort Tompkins, successive landings of British troops on Horse Island create a viable bridgehead (1) and advance across the island (1a). The advance of this force (100th Regiment) makes a sustained bayonet charge across the partially submerged causeway (1b, T) directly at the line of American entrenchments and troops lining the mainland shore. In response, the American militia units manning these positions rout, many almost without firing a shot (1c, 1d, 1e) and flee into the woods. Other units make a semi-disciplined retreat down the shoreline (1f, 1g, 1h, 1i) to link-up with the troops manning the line of abattis (1j) on the road leading to the village.

2. After securing their positions on the mainland, the British force advances in column down the main track leading along the shoreline toward the village (2, 2a). This column then divides at a split in the trail, with the left column (8th [Kings] Regiment, 100th, Royal Newfoundland Regiment, and Glengarry Light Infantry) following the waterside trail and adjacent ground (2b) while the right column (104th, Canadian Voltigeurs, Native Warriors) are detached inland (east) in pursuit of the fleeing American militias and to secure the British right flank (2c). As the right column advances, the broken ground and wooded trail, coupled with the dispersed nature of the enemy, results in a further

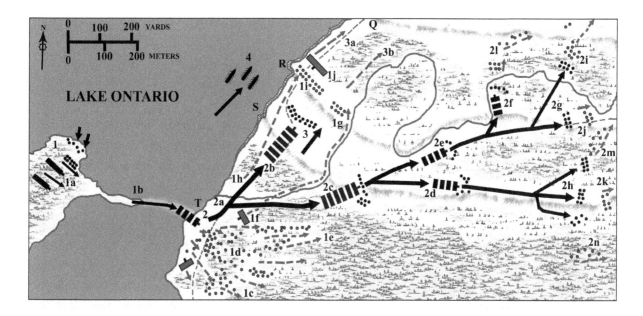

division of the column's forces, with the Voltigeurs and Natives moving further to the right (2d) and the 104th swinging to the left (2e). Continuing to advance, these units are further broken into separate detachments, advancing independently on a wide and disorganized front (2f, 2g, 2h). In response, detachments of U.S. militia make occasional defensive stands (2i, 1i, 2j) before continuing their retreat, but the bulk of the American militia on this flank continue their routed retreat away from the fighting and are dispersed (2l, 2m, 2n).

3. The British left column, advancing along the waterside trail (3), encounters stiff resistance from detachments of militia and regulars (1g, 1i, 1j) manning the middle defensive abattis (R). Taking casualties, the British press forward, forcing the American units to make a fighting withdrawal back toward the village and Fort Tompkins (3a, 3b).

4. Offshore, the British gunboats (4), intended to provide fire support for the landings, find their guns cannot elevate sufficiently to clear the obstruction of the line of low waterside cliffs (that line the shore) and are thus unable to successfully target the exposed flank of the American units making a stand against the advancing British forces.

this onslaught of cold steel, despite having the advantage of firepower and defensive positions, the relatively untrained American militiamen increasingly saw their military role in the conflict as concluded and proceeded in ones, tens, then entire sections to abandon their posts and head for the nearby woods with all speed. Only a few even attempted to fire their weapons, while those who initially stood their ground soon found themselves defending positions that were untenable and either joined the rout or retired back toward the succeeding lines of American troops stationed nearer the Basswood Cantonment barracks and Fort Tompkins.

Previously supremely confident of his self-proclaimed expertise in establishing his defensive positions and seeing his predictions initially fulfilled as to the point of British landing, Brigadier General Brown saw his plans disintegrate before his eyes. In his own words:

> Not a shot was fired from their column, the front approaching charging bayonets....
>
> To my utter astonishment, my men arose from their cover and broke & before I could realize the disgraceful scene, there was scarcely a man within several rods of where I stood ... I made all the noise I could for my men, put my handkerchief on the point of my sword and made every sort of signal possible that they might notice, but in vain....[7]

Recognizing that the initial encounter was irrevocably lost, Brown quickly mounted his horse and joined his men in putting distance between himself and the enemy.

With the causeway and beachhead secure, the British continued to advance, but were soon slowed by the combined fire of American artillery from Fort Tompkins, the thick entanglements of the lines of abattis flanking the American positions, defensive fire from units of militia that had reformed under cover of the abattis, and a distinct lack of their own artillery support. This latter factor was the combined result of the main British fleet remaining becalmed well out of firing range, the supporting gunboats carrying artillery pieces that could not elevate sufficiently to provide fire support, and the blunder of putting the land artillery pieces in one set of boats and the crews in another, neither of which was anywhere near reaching the shore. There was also an unfortunate instance of friendly fire upon the 104th Regiment by men of the Lower Canada Voltigeur Regiment. This regiment had been one of the last units to land, and under the prevailing conditions of poor visibility (due to the heavy gunsmoke hanging in the damp and still morning air) they had been unable to determine the status of the events taking place before them. As a result, one overly excited officer (Captain William Johnson) did not take the time to properly identify the body of troops to his front, and simply fired his command into the backs of the indistinct shape. He was soon told, in no uncertain and unflattering terms, of his catastrophic blunder by the victim regiment's commanding officer, Major William Drummond.

Looking to regain the initiative, the main body of attackers, consisting of the 8th (Kings), 100th, Royal Newfoundland, and Glengarry Light Infantry Regiments, led by Colonel Young (8th [King's] Regiment), moved along the trackway running at the edge of the low cliffs toward the Basswood Cantonment and Fort Tompkins. At the same time a second body, consisting of the 104th, Canadian Voltigeurs, and Native warriors under Major Drummond (104th), were detached with orders to move to their right and approach the village from that quadrant. Shortly thereafter this column also subdivided, with the Voltigeurs and Natives moving even further to the right with orders to press any defenders making a stand among the undergrowth of the woodlands and lines of abattis and secure the flank of the main British thrust. Because of the broken and entangled nature of the terrain

on this flank, this force soon found itself broken into small detachments, each taking its own line of advance and fighting its own battle with whatever defenders chose to make a stand..

On the American side of the field, with the militia contingent collapsed and on the run and General Brown nowhere to be found, command of the support troops and remaining defensive positions fell to Lieutenant Colonel Backus once again. Advancing his reserves from the cantonment, and backed by Lieutenant Louis Laval and his 6-pounder artillery piece, as well as some of the retreating militia, Backus established a new line of defensive fire along the inner line of abattis that began to take a steady and increasing toll upon the advancing British force. However, despite putting up a stout and brave resistance, the determined advances of the British on the flanks and equally deadly return fire forced the Americans to begin a fighting retreat back toward Fort Tompkins. Meanwhile, away from the fighting, General Brown later claimed he was otherwise occupied in an attempt to reform some semblance of a militia force that could then rejoin the action and bolster the American line. Unfortunately, he found that there was considerable reluctance on the part of many detachments to rejoin the engagement. While those who did initially appear willing, they quickly dispersed when they encountered parties

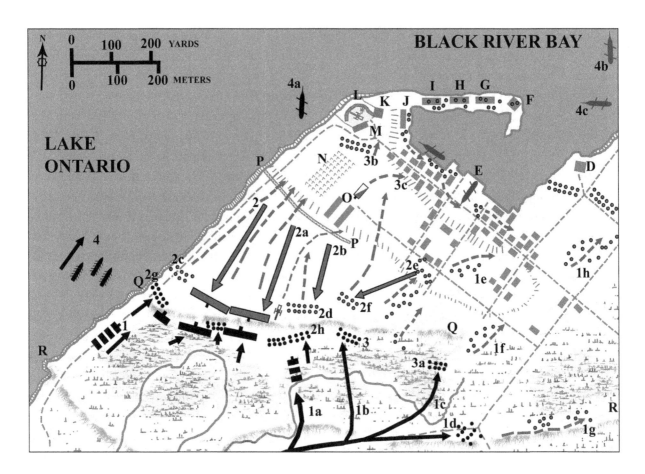

THE FIGHT FOR THE ABATTIS LINES (6:30–7:45 a.m.)

D   Blockhouse
E   Naval dockyard (with the future *General Pike*
    under construction on the stocks, and the *Duke
    of Gloucester*, previously captured at York, at the
    quayside)
F   Navy Point, Blockhouse

G   Navy Point, Lower Artillery Battery/Barracks/
    Storehouse
H   Navy Point, Middle Artillery Battery/Barracks/
    Storehouse
I   Navy Point, Upper Artillery Battery/Barracks/
    Storehouse

J   Warehouse
K   Fort Tompkins, Blockhouse
L   Fort Tompkins Artillery Battery (32-pounder)
M   Fort Tompkins, Marine Barracks
N   Tented encampment
O   Basswood Cantonment Barracks
P   Drainage ditch
Q   Inner line of abattis (*constructed late spring 1813)
R   Middle line of abattis (*constructed February 1813, incomplete and overgrown)

1. The British Left column (1) and separate elements of the right column (1a, 1b, 1c) press forward against varying degrees of opposition by units of Americans fighting from the cover of the abattis lines (R, Q) and thick underbrush. On the far right flank, British Native allies (1d) continue their sweep around the east side of the village, as routed American militias continue their retreat from the battlefield (1e, 1f, 1g, 1h).

2. U.S. Colonel Backus orders the advance of his main reserve (detachments of Ninth and Twenty-Third Infantry regiments, First Light Dragoons regiment (unmounted), and one 6-pounder and crew) (2, 2a, 2b) to bolster the American positions along the inner abattis line (Q), producing a line-of-battle (2c, 2d) that is reinforced by returning detachments of reformed American militia (2e, 2f). The British advance stalls in the face of this strengthened opposition and, after forming a line of their own (2g, 2h), a battle ensues at almost point-blank range, inflicting heavy casualties on both sides.

3. Under increasing pressure and with their left wing in danger of being outflanked by advancing units of the British right column (3, 3a), the American line initiates a fighting withdrawal back to the Basswood cantonment (O) and adjacent drainage ditch (P), where they begin to establish a new line of defence. Units in reserve (3b) and the mounted cavalry (First Light Dragoons and detachments of mounted militia) (3c) also begin to retire.

4. Offshore, the British gunboats (4) maintain a relatively ineffective artillery fire on the American units that can be seen nearest the cliff top. The *Beresford* (4a), the only vessel from the British fleet to move inshore, engages in counter battery fire with Fort Tompkins (L), setting alight the nearby barracks (M) that temporarily halts the American main gun's firing. In addition, overshots from the *Beresford* land along the line of the harbour warehouse (J) and warehouse/barracks/artillery positions on Navy Point (G, H, I) panicking their gun crews into believing Fort Tompkins had fallen and the British were firing down upon them and causing some gun crews to abandon their positions. The U.S. vessels, *Fair American* and *Pert* (4b, 4c), are ordered to weigh anchor and proceed north to escape capture.

of British troops, Voltigeurs, and Natives active on that part of the battlefield.

Behind the American lines, the defenders assigned to man the artillery batteries at Navy Point and Fort Volunteer had remained relatively inactive throughout the morning as the increasingly louder sounds of battle drifted back from over the hill, indicating that the British were gaining ground. The two vessels, *Fair American* and *Pert*, had already been ordered by Lieutenant Wolcott Chauncey (brother to Commodore Chauncey and senior naval officer at the harbour) to use their long sweep oars to propel themselves out of the harbour and off to the north to avoid being trapped by the British fleet. Now, with the main British flotilla sitting idly well out of firing range, the only British naval presence fell to the gunboats and HMS *Beresford*, a former merchant topsail schooner adapted to carry ten 18-pounder carronades and two long 9-pounders. This vessel had been laboriously rowed in under fire from the American gun positions until it was positioned off the exposed flank of Fort Tompkins and directly in line with the left flank of the batteries on Navy Point. Once the *Beresford* opened fire it ignited the Marine Barracks behind the large 32-pounder in Fort Tomkins. So hot did this fire become that the gun had to be abandoned, temporarily ending its damaging bombardment of the British troops. In addition, any rounds that overshot Fort Tompins

landed among the crews of the Navy Point batteries, persuading them that Fort Tompkins had fallen and its guns were now trained on them, precipitating a cascade abandonment of these otherwise strong artillery positions by their crews. As a result, the *Beresford* was able to move round the point and opened fire directly into the heart of the port.

Moving slowly up the bay under oars, the *Fair American* and *Pert* exchanged a long-range passing fire with the *Beresford* but made no attempt to seriously engage her. Under this flanking fire, and with deserters and casualties coming back from both Navy Point and the fighting over the hill indicating that the British had either taken Fort Tompkins or the Americans were abandoning the position, the secondary orders left by Commodore Chauncey and reiterated by Lieutenant Chauncey (now sailing up the bay in the *Fair American)* were implemented by his subordinates, Master Commandant Leonard, Joseph Gamble, Sailing Master Hutton, and Lieutenant Drury. These prior orders stated that in the event of a British attack actually overrunning the American defences or appearing to carry the garrison a red flag would be raised and then lowered aboard the *Fair American*. Upon seeing this command, all of the battery artillery positions were to be spiked, the warehouses and other military structures were to be set on fire, and the vessels in the harbour were to be scuttled or fired to deny their use to the enemy. Although there were procedures to prevent any accidental or premature implementation of these last-resort orders, the defeatist reports coming back from the battlefield, plus the subsequent sworn testimonies of those at several locations that the red flag was indeed raised and lowered aboard the *Fair American*, led to the implementation of the self-destruct instructions. As a result, despite Lieutenant Chauncey's later vehement denial that he had raised the red-flag order, the torches were set and the buildings began to burn.

Back on the main battlefield, the American defensive line was under great strain and suffering casualties, but it had not broken. However, with all of his available effective troops committed and pushed back to the American entrenchments, it was not long before Lieutenant Colonel Backus decided to order his line to retire on Fort Volunteer. As the American troops began to disengage and pull back, Backus received a mortal wound and command fell upon Major Laval, who confirmed the retreat orders. Inside Fort Tompkins, however, the artillerists manning the guns, backed by the remnants of the Ninth and Twenty-First Infantry, remained in place and continued the engagement, while infantry stragglers and elements of the First Dragoons either joined the now isolated garrison inside the fort or fled through the town, spreading alarm and panic. A British victory and the fall of the harbour seemed inevitable.

What the Americans did not know was that the British offensive was slowly but surely running out of steam, as its casualties mounted. By now the depleted remnants of the British attacking force had finally reached the Basswood Cantonment and, using its cover, had made several attempts to storm the Fort Tompkins position. But after fierce point-blank firing, they were driven off each time by the determined resistance of the ad hoc defending garrison.

Behind the British line, Sir George Prevost had been with the main body throughout the day's action. As the titular senior officer, he was in command of the entire British battle strategy and execution. Unfortunately, Prevost was first and foremost an administrative commander and, compared to some of his subordinates, relatively inexperienced in battlefield command situations. From his perspective, his command had suffered crippling numbers of casualties from enemy fire while the expected artillery support of his naval contingent was sitting idly offshore, contributing nothing to the attack. To his front, while most of the enemy's forces had retreated from the field, its principal fortification was stubbornly holding out and blocking his advance to gain his ultimate objective of the harbour. As such, he had had no way of knowing that the Americans on the other side of the rise in

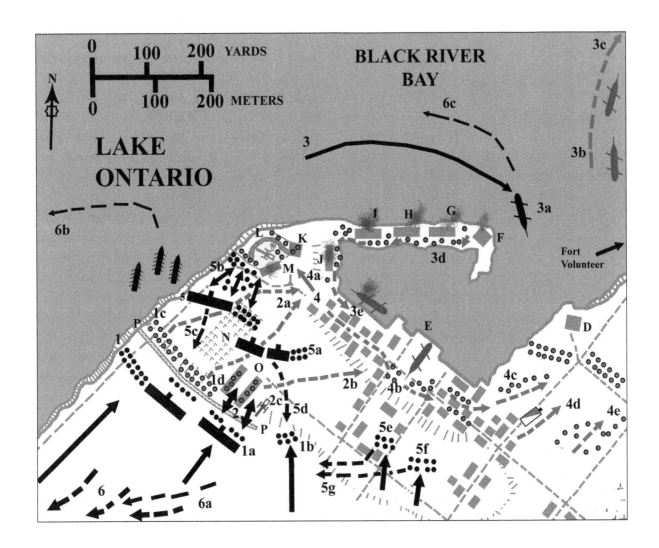

THE FIGHT FOR FORT TOMPKINS, THE AMERICAN DESTRUCTION OF THEIR OWN POSITIONS, AND THE FINAL BRITISH RETREAT (7:45–8:30 a.m.)

D   Blockhouse
E   Naval dockyard (with the future *General Pike* under construction on the stocks, and the *Duke of Gloucester*, previously captured at York, at the quayside)
F   Navy Point, Blockhouse
G   Navy Point, Lower Artillery Battery/Barracks/Storehouse
H   Navy Point, Middle Artillery Battery/Barracks/Storehouse
I   Navy Point, Upper Artillery Battery/Barracks/Storehouse
J   Warehouse
K   Fort Tompkins, Blockhouse
L   Fort Tompkins Artillery Battery (32-pounder)
M   Fort Tompkins, Marine Barracks
N   Tented encampment
O   Basswood Cantonment Barracks
P   Drainage ditch

1. The British line advances and forms a new line-of-battle (1, 1a), while units farther to the right (1b) move round to flank the American line (1c, 1d) stationed along the drainage ditch (P) and inside the Basswood Cantonment Barracks (O).

2. Elements of the British line make repeated unsuccessful assaults upon the American troops occupying the Basswood Cantonment Barracks (2, O). Following additional heavy fighting, the American line is forced to retreat toward Fort Tompkins and the village, where they begin to regroup (2a). Units inside the Basswood Cantonment barracks are also forced to abandon their positions and retreat toward the village (2b), leaving behind their only field artillery piece to be captured by the British (2c).

3. Offshore, having silenced the guns in Fort Topkins (L), the *Beresford* sails around Navy Point (3, 3a), enfilading the position with its fire. It also engages the retreating American vessels *Fair American and Pert* (3b, 3c). On Navy Point the remaining defenders (artillery, navy crews, and dockyard workers) (3d), believing that Fort Tompkins has fallen and the American line has collapsed, now claim they see the signal from the *Fair American* to destroy their positions. They therefore set about igniting the Navy Point defences (F, G, H, I) and make a rapid retreat through the village (3e), igniting fires at the main warehouse (J), the *Duke of Gloucester*, and shipyard (E).

4. In the ground between Fort Tompkins (L) and the village, detachments and remnants of units gather to make a final stand (4), when orders come to continue the retreat to Fort Volunteer. Some detachments ignore these orders and blockade themselves inside Fort Tompkins (4a), while others fall back through the village (4b, 4c, 4d, 4e) toward Fort Volunteer (off map) leaving the Fort Tompkins detachments isolated.

5. The British units on the left of the line advance toward Fort Tompkins (5, 5a) and repeated attempts are made to storm the fort (5b), but without success. Unable to see over the rise in ground into the harbour and faced with the resistance of Fort Tompkins, General Prevost decides to make an initial short withdrawal (5c, 5d) and regroup back near the drainage ditch (P). On the right flank, detached units (5e, 5f), who can see the American retreat and burning buildings are frustrated by the recall, but obey and move back (5g) toward the British main body.

6. General Prevost makes the unilateral decision to abandon the attack and withdraw (6, 6a). The gunboats and the *Beresford* break off and retire (6b, 6c) back to the main British fleet.

ground were in full flight and beginning to do his work of destruction for him. He also had no reconnaissance information about what was occurring on his right flank or in the area beyond his immediate vision, leaving open the potential that the longer he was delayed, the more likely that the Americans were going to receive reinforcements and make a counterattack upon his position. There was also the possibility that because of the delay of over twenty-four hours in making the initial attack, Commodore Chauncey's fleet might appear on the horizon, cutting off his line of retreat to Kingston aboard his waiting flotilla. Under these conditions, Prevost personally ordered the cessation of the attack and the sounding of the recall for all units.

Despite their shock at hearing the call to retreat at what seemed the moment of victory, the disciplined British soldiers obeyed their orders and began to fall back, surrendering the hard-won ground without a fight. As the British line assembled out of firing range of the American defenders, hoping for the opportunity to make one more concerted attack by the entire remaining force, Major Drummond personally went forward under a flag of truce and called for the Americans to surrender. Despite being almost out of ammunition and with only a few unwounded men to man the walls, Major Laval met Drummond's call with defiance, correctly assessing that the bugle calls and British withdrawal signalled a weakness in the British resolve to continue the action. Hearing of Laval's defiance from Major Drummond, Sir George Prevost made the decision to terminate all operations and ordered his force to retreat to their boats. Upon being pressed by Major Drummond to make one final push and not abandon the fruits of the victory already attained, Prevost rebuked his subordinate, reminding him of his primary duty to obey his superiors' orders and demanded the retreat begin immediately.

Across the field, the British and Canadian units heard the sounds of the bugle calling retreat with varying degrees of astonishment and frustrated anger. Some were in a position to see the dockyards burning and the Americans in full flight. Initially they could not fathom the need for a withdrawal and so only reluctantly obeyed. Other units, interpreting that the order meant American reinforcements were arriving, or a major counterattack was about to take place, made off toward the boats with speed — a situation that soon transmuted their nonexistent danger into a panicked imagining of imminent disaster. This unfettered rumour quickly transmitted itself to other units and turned the orderly withdrawal of Prevost's forces into a partial rout, with the Americans in Fort Tompkins watching in astonishment as the all-but-triumphant enemy melted away before them.

Back on the landing beaches, discipline amongst the returning troops had almost collapsed. Prompted by the wild rumours, weapons and supplies were abandoned as the men sought places in the shuttle of boats returning to the flotilla. Such was the disorder of this re-embarkation that several units of late-comers and the rearguard found themselves stranded without boats, forcing them to search for their own evacuation transport, which they eventually found, returning to the British flotilla around 9:00 a.m.[*8]

With the British in full retreat, some of the American mounted dragoon commanders, who had played little significant part in the day's events, wanted to initiate an immediate pursuit. However, to their annoyance, Major Laval vetoed this idea and ordered all units to remain in position and secure the defensive perimeter of the harbour. Likewise, within the harbour itself, once the *Beresford* was seen to be retreating toward the flotilla, the *Fair American* and *Pert* started rowing back toward Fort Volunteer and the docks, while volunteer crews from the yard began to extinguish the fires in order to salvage as much as possible from total destruction. Only then did General Brown reappear on the field. Reviewing the situation and deciding that the British were definitely abandoning the offensive, Brown rode off once again to cajole the reluctant militia formations gathered outside the village to return to their posts and help salvage the dockyard

warehouses. He also made sure that he composed the first official report on the day's action, with copies going to the secretary of war and Governor Tompkins. In these documents, while he gave credit to the strong defensive stand made by the regular army troops at Fort Tompkins, he also phrased the remainder of the affair to reflect the maximum credit upon himself as the architect of what he claimed was a major American victory.

ESTIMATED CASUALTIES, BATTLE OF SACKETS HARBOR, MAY 29, 1813[*8]

British

Killed: 1 deputy assistant quartermaster general, 47 other ranks
Wounded: 12 officers, 2 drummers, 179 other ranks, 2 artillery gunners
Missing/Prisoners: 3 officers, 13 other ranks
Naval Losses: 1 killed, 6 wounded, all ranks

American

Regulars
Killed: 1 officer, 20 other ranks
Wounded: 5 officers, 79 other ranks

Militias
Killed: 1 other ranks
Wounded: 21 other ranks
Missing/Prisoner: 26 other ranks

In the aftermath of the battle of Sackets Harbor, both sides were forced to make significant changes in their future campaign strategies. The after-effects of this action also held a significant place upon the future decisions and actions of the senior commanders on both sides of the border.

For Sir George Prevost, his return to Kingston was initially hailed by its citizens as the return of a conquering hero. However, this quickly turned to shock and dismay once they heard the unwelcome news that the expedition had failed. During the next few days this shock changed into a swelling backlash of personal criticism upon Sir George, especially once the eye-witness survivors told their versions of how a hard-won near victory had been turned into a panicked and humiliating defeat at the last moment — apparently exclusively by the commands of their inexperienced battlefield commander. Furthermore, the losses in manpower and resources at Sackets Harbor had compromised the effective fighting capabilities of the vital Kingston position, making it vulnerable to an American attack until reinforcements could be brought up from Lower Canada. Finally, news arrived from General Vincent reporting on the American successful invasion and the British Army's retreat toward Burlington Heights. This brought the crisis of the threat on the Niagara into instant focus and made the necessity of sending Vincent reinforcements even more vital, even if it meant stripping Kingston of even more of its weakened garrison.

From Prevost's perspective, it now became necessary, nay vital that he engage in some damage control. In order of priority, he first needed to ensure that his dubious command decisions at Sackets Harbor be seen in the best possible light by his superiors, second that he silence his local critics, and thirdly, that he deal with the crisis on the Niagara. He began by writing his official account of events to Earl Bathurst in London, dated June 1, 1813. This communique (Bulletin No. 64) became a carefully phrased document that began by claiming that the expedition was not an attack to destroy the American base, but merely a deliberate diversionary show of force to disrupt the American activities on the Niagara and assist Vincent. In addition, he overestimated both the American troop numbers and the state of American defences to explain his troop losses and justify his decision to withdraw. He also attempted to shift some of the blame onto Sir James Yeo, by inferring that he (Prevost) knew nothing about the absence of the fleet until late in the battle (when in reality they were fully visible to Sir George throughout the action) and that the heavy troop losses and the failure of the "diversion" were therefore partially due to the failure of the fleet to provide the required artillery support to the landings.

Altho' as Your Lordship will perceive … the expedition has not been attended with the complete success which has been expected from it, I have the great satisfaction in informing Your Lordship that the courage and patience of the small band of troops employed on this occasion, under circumstances of peculiar hardship and privation, have been exceeded only by their intrepid conduct in the field, forcing a passage at the point of the bayonet through a thickly wooded country, affording constant shelter and strong positions to the enemy, but not a single spot of ground favourable to the operations of disciplined soldiers. The enemy filled the woods with infantry supported by field pieces, and kept up a heavy and destructive fire which could not, however stop the determined advance of His Majesty's troops … who drove far superior numbers by a spirited charge to seek shelter within their blockhouses and enclosed works. At this moment the enemy were induced to burn their storehouses, but a heavier fire than that of musketry having become necessary in order to force their last position, I had the mortification to learn that the continuation of light and adverse winds had prevented the co-operation of the ships, and that the gunboats were unequal to silence the enemy's elevated battery or to produce any effect on their blockhouses. Considering it therefore impracticable without such assistance to carry the strong works by which the post was defended, I reluctantly ordered the troops to leave a beaten enemy whom they had driven before them for upwards of three hours, and whom did not venture to offer the slightest opposition to the re-embarkation, which was effected with proper deliberation and in perfect order.[9]

To deal with his local critics, while there is no direct documented evidence that he may have looked to divert criticism away from himself, the following sequence of timing remains suspiciously convenient. Having previously maintained a steadfast support of Major General Sir Roger Sheaffe against the complaints of those same civilian critics, Prevost suddenly reversed his position and issued the following terse statement in the publicly viewed General Orders, dated June 6, 1813.

> Major-General De Rottenburg will deliver over the command of the troops and the civil administration of the

Province of Lower Canada to Major-General Glasgow, and is to arrive at Kingston on the 20th inst. Major-General Sir R. Sheaffe will meet Major General De Rottenburg at Cornwall on the 15th and from thence proceed to Montreal to assume the command of the troops in that district.[10]

Interestingly, although Prevost had made a private mention of the need to make this replacement prior to the Sackets Harbor engagement (bulletin No. 63 to Earl Bathurst) on May 26, he had also specifically stated that this would only take place once the military situation on the Niagara had settled down, he had completed his reinforcement of General Vincent, and had received an approval confirmation of his intention from London. Now the change was pushed through without delay, and Prevost did not see fit to include this very significant item of news in his subsequent official communiqués to Earl Bathurst. In fact, it was not until Bulletin No. 72 dated June 24, 1813, after writing: "I have the honour to transmit to Your Lordship a copy of a public declaration given out by the American commandant of Fort Erie, after the enemy had taken possession of that post, and the proclamation which I deemed it necessary to issue in consequence of it,"[11] that Prevost dismissingly broached the subject of his unilateral entire change in command in Upper Canada.

I avail myself of this opportunity of informing Your Lordship that finding upon my arrival at this place [which, in fact, had been almost two months earlier] that Major-General Sir Roger Sheaffe had altogether lost the confidence of the Province by the measures he had pursued for its defence, I deemed it most conducive to the good of the public service to remove that officer to Montreal and to Substitute Major-General De Rottenburg in his place.[12]

Finally, to deal with the issue on the Niagara, Prevost began to muster a relief force and supplies that would need transportation aboard Yeo's fleet if it was to arrive with any hope of being in time to assist Vincent. Unfortunately, Yeo's co-operation on the matter was something of a question at that moment.

For Sir James Yeo, the expedition to Sackets Harbor had been a severe test of his command abilities. To his credit he had successfully mounted an amphibious expedition in less than twenty-four hours, only a fortnight after taking up his new command, and with no real knowledge of the capabilities of his ships or crews. He had maintained the integrity of his fleet under variable weather conditions, suffered negligible losses during the course of the action, and brought his command home intact. On the other hand, while he was perhaps justified in exercising a degree of caution in view of his unfamiliarity with the waters, the uncertain weather, and the variable winds his fleet experienced, the fact that he personally went ashore and participated in the action, instead of supervising the movement of his fleet inshore to bombard the American positions, definitely left Yeo open to criticism — which was not helped by Prevost's version of events and implied blame. In the aftermath of the events of May 28th, a series of communications took place between the two commanders, as well as from the two to their masters in London, about the relative degrees of responsibility for the failure of the expedition. This inevitably cooled and then soured relations between Sir George and Sir James for some time to come — just when the maximum degree of support and co-operation was needed in the British camp.

For Commodore Chauncey, when the *Lady of the Lake* arrived at the Niagara River (late on May 29th) bearing the alarming news that the British fleet had sailed, he was placed in a dilemma. The report did not contain any detailed information about the destination of the British flotilla, but it was evident that Sackets Harbor was a potential priority target. On the other hand, there was also the possibility that Yeo's goal was to break through with reinforcements for Vincent and take on the American fleet while it was hamstrung in its manoeuvring by the need to maintain contact with Dearborn's land forces. In addition, by his own orders, several vessels had been detached to make reconnaissance sweeps around the west end of the lake, thus leaving his fighting force reduced in firepower if the British appeared. Consequently, Chauncey notified Dearborn that effective immediately, he intended to leave and seek out the enemy fleet before returning to protect his naval base. He also pressured Dearborn to supply troops to augment the Sackets Harbor garrison. In reply, Dearborn detached 200 men, under Colonel Macomb, to travel with Chauncey, while Lieutenant Colonel Ripley and his regiment were ordered to march to the harbour by way of Oswego. However, despite the urgency of the moment, Chauncey was forced to wait over twenty-four hours until his vessels returned before sailing north toward York and the northern shore of Lake Ontario — it being the most likely route Yeo and Proctor would take if their intention was to link up with Vincent. When no enemy appeared, Chauncey set course for Kingston and Sackets

Harbor with all sail. After locating the enemy back in port at Kingston, Chauncey reached his base late in the afternoon of June 1st.

Upon his arrival, Commodore Chauncey found that while most of the dockyard and the hull of his new warship had been saved from destruction, the same could not be said for the barracks and warehouses on Navy Point, which not only contained the fittings and supplies that were needed to finish her off and make her fit for sea but also the entire stock of captured supplies from York. Although Brigadier General Brown was in titular command, the post was in a state of virtual anarchy with no one, least of all Brown, taking the responsibility to coordinate repairs and see to the needs of the numerous detachments of militia and regulars who had descended on the port in the aftermath of the alert. In fact, within a short time after Chauncey and Macomb's arrival, Brown had not only relinquished his command to Macomb but, instead of remaining to support the two officers, immediately left for his own community at Brownsville, a little way up the shoreline — leaving the two returnees to clean up the chaos of the moment, while he made sure that his version of the events surrounding the battle became public knowledge through leaks to the press.

While Colonel Macomb took charge of the reorganization of the base's defences, Commodore Chauncey was left to deal with the political fallout of the near disaster and the inevitable blame game that flared up between the various participants. Major Laval found himself criticized and condemned by other officers for ordering the retreat to Fort Volunteer when the Americans seemed defeated and then not allowing a pursuit of the British when they, in turn, retreated. Similarly Lieutenant Chauncey, along with his subordinates Master Commandant Leonard, Joseph Gamble, Sailing Master Hutton, and Lieutenant Drury, were all accused of various offences. These included cowardice and dereliction of duty (for having the warehouses burned) and permitting the defences at Navy Point to be abandoned without any direct attack taking place on that position in contravention of orders.

Left with no option but to convene a court of inquiry, Commodore Chauncey personally selected the judges. Once empanelled, the judges quickly concluded that Major Laval had been justified in his command decisions and the officer was acquitted on all charges. In the case of Lieutenant Chauncey and his subordinates, however, more complicated issues were involved and testimonies were entered clearly implicating all four men. Suspiciously, the panel's subsequent findings exonerated the lieutenant but found the remainder culpable. This led to the dismissal of Leonard,

Gamble, and Hutton. In the case of Lieutenant Drury, while the initial findings of Chauncey's hand-picked inquiry also held him guilty, testimonies given at his subsequent (and more independent) court martial not only contradicted the prior findings but also began to expose additional damaging details of Lieutenant Chauncey's behaviour, orders, and actions during the day's events. Before this line of inquiry had continued too far the court was summarily adjourned and almost immediately came back with a finding of not guilty on the major counts of disobedience of orders and cowardice. However, Drury was censured on a lesser infraction, leading to a private reprimand being put on his record by the commodore and, during the course of the following year, was repeatedly passed over for promotion while still under the command of that senior officer.

In addition, for Commodore Chauncey the near catastrophe of losing his new and still unnamed vessel, not to mention his entire base of operations, coupled with the actual loss of all the supplies intended to fit her out, left him determined to secure her completion and inclusion in his Lake Ontario fleet. Despite the fact that obtaining replacement supplies and completing the vessel would take at least a month or more, Chauncey made the decision that not only was he going to remain at Sackets Harbor to personally oversee the project to its completion, but that his entire fleet would remain there as well, for protection. Despite requests and then pleas from his captains to let them venture out under separate or independent commands to harass the enemy, Chauncey was determined that only *he* would lead his fleet and restricted them to either remaining at the harbour or being dispatched as picket vessels to guard the approaches to the harbour. As a result, the throttle-hold the Americans had on the British supply lines was suddenly and unilaterally released — a situation that the British were quick to take advantage of.

For Brigadier General Jacob Brown, the aftermath of the battle at Sackets Harbor was one of opportunity and advantage. Easily the most adept "political" general in American service, he avoided the negative inferences and implications revealed at the court of inquiry by making sure that he remained distinctly absent from the scene. He also made sure that his official reports were copied and distributed to most of the relevant political personalities in Washington, D.C., as well as the press. As a result, his credentials as the "saviour" of Sackets Harbor became such a matter of "known fact" that those who believed anything different found it in their own best interests not to challenge the instant celebrity of Brown, at least for the moment.

In addition, although Brigadier General Brown had already declined a previous official offer of a transfer from the militia to the regular army (because under the standard terms of this kind of transfer it would necessitate him losing his rank of general and being reduced to colonel), Brown used his celebrity status to parlay the "victory" into getting a transfer directly to the regular army *without* any loss of rank or seniority. This singular occurrence, made at the direction of the president, not only broke precedence and military protocols but was also, naturally, taken as a "slap in the face" for those regulars who were nominally next in line for promotion. This special treatment led to a strong degree of resentment against Brown within the corps of regular army officers. A resentment that was still very evident more than a year later when he commanded the Northern Army on the Niagara.

As for the effect the battle of Sackets Harbor had on the course of the campaign to control the Niagara frontier — it took less than a fortnight before the pendulum began to swing in an entirely new direction, halting the sweep of American victories thus far achieved.

CHAPTER 6

Confusion in the Darkness:
The Battle of Stoney Creek, June 6, 1813

Following what was later criticized as an inordinate delay, the American pursuit of the retreating British on the Niagara frontier finally began at dawn on June 1, 1813. Commanded by Brigadier General Winder, the original plan had been for Chauncey's fleet to sail down the lake in conjunction with this land force, but with its abrupt departure, it left the army without the navy's logistical, transport, and firepower support for the remainder of the campaign. In addition, by failing to order a proper reconnaissance that would have quickly revealed that the British rearguard only consisted of a detachment of Provincial Light Dragoons, Winder's force made a cautious advance down the main Black Swamp trail that ran across the plain below the escarpment. This also put him under constant observation by parties of Native warriors,

Incorporated Militia, and Embodied Militia on the commanding heights to the south. Nor did the weather co-operate, as a succession of rainstorms reduced the main road into a mud-choked quagmire, slowing the already slow American advance to a crawl that eventually reached the Forty Mile Creek on the morning of June 2nd, whereupon it halted and established an encampment.

At the same time, General Dearborn revised his plans yet again by ordering Brigadier General Chandler to march with an additional brigade to join Winder. Departing Fort George on June 3rd, Chandler reached the Forty Mile Creek on the morning of the 5th, fully expecting that Winder's force would have already departed and was actively engaged in pressing the British towards Burlington Heights. Instead, he found it sitting idly awaiting his arrival. Uniting the forces and taking overall command, Chandler ordered that the advance continue without further delay. After skirmishing throughout the afternoon of the 5th, with an augmented British rearguard made up of the Light Dragoons and a detachment of the 49th Regiment, supported by the units of militia and Native warriors from the escarpment, the American advance guard had almost reached Burlington Heights. However, with night drawing on, it was recalled to join the main body of some 3,200 troops in the area now defined as Stoney Creek. Despite the known proximity of the British base, the American troops were positioned along an extended line that stretched from the escarpment to the lake, a front of around two miles (3.5 kilometers). Inevitably, gaps and weak spots in the defensive perimeter developed. Even within the main body of troops that encamped in the fields of the William and James Gage farmsteads, no directives on regimental alignment or rallying points came from either of the commanding generals, as it was anticipated that if the British made any stand it would be during the following day, once the Americans approached Burlington Heights. Instead, the individual regimental placements were left to the discretion of their commanding officers, which, according to their individual levels of military skill, varied from sensible to foolhardy.

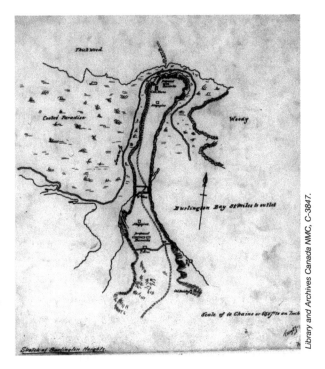

Library and Archives Canada NMC, C-3847.

A British map of the defences established at the strategic transportation and supply hub of Burlington Heights (Hamilton).

The result was that the American force became dispersed across the undulating and broken ground below the dominating escarpment. It also failed to make more than a rudimentary plan of defence that centred along the line of a low, split-rail fence, topping a brush-covered ridge of ground that ran north-south to the east of the

James Gage farmstead and intersected with the main east-west road to the north of the house. The clear field of fire created by the road and a stretch of low open ground was seen as the optimum location to deploy part of Towson's artillery and pitch the general's headquarters tent. Otherwise, camp discipline was so lax that the Twenty-Fifth Regiment set up its camp in front of the American line, directly obstructing Towson's field of fire. This regiment further ignored established camp regulations by starting cooking campfires within their tent lines. On the other hand, some regimental officers sought to take precautions against a possible nighttime harassing probe by the enemy. For example, when Lieutenant John Kearsley (later major, Fourth U.S. Rifle Regiment) was instructed to establish a picket line at a small Methodist chapel, located about 500 yards (300 meters) in front of the American lines with men of

> Maj. Forsyth's riflemen, two companies
> of the 22nd Infantry and four companies
> of the 2nd Artillery ... [he] ... remon-
> strated against selecting these troops; first
> because they were exceptionally fatigued
> from the severe duties and fighting dur-
> ing the day, to which the other troops
> had not been exposed; and more espe-
> cially because the Riflemen of Forsyth

had never been disciplined to picket guard duty, and would therefore, probably, wherever they might be stationed, lie down and go to sleep. The Brigade Major, Captain Roger Jones, however persisted in his demand and Maj. Kearsley personally visited Genl. Chandler and remonstrated against ... confiding the army to the keeping of troops who, in the language of Maj. Forsyth, "had never performed guard duty in their life." Gen. Chandler however replied "that his arrangements for the night had been made and could not be changed".... A company of the Riflemen under Capt. Van Swearengen ... took up their quarters in the church and went comfortably to sleep in the pews thereof.[1]

At the same time, Major Joseph Smith (Twenty-Fifth Regiment) was having second thoughts about his unit's relatively exposed location and despite having his tents pitched, his men settled and many already asleep, he requested a repositioning of his regiment. Assured by his commanders that no threat existed, Smith badgered Chandler and Winder until they relented and let him relocate his troops to a position alongside Towson's artillery, leaving behind most of the tents and cooking fires to the supervision of a detachment of cooks and

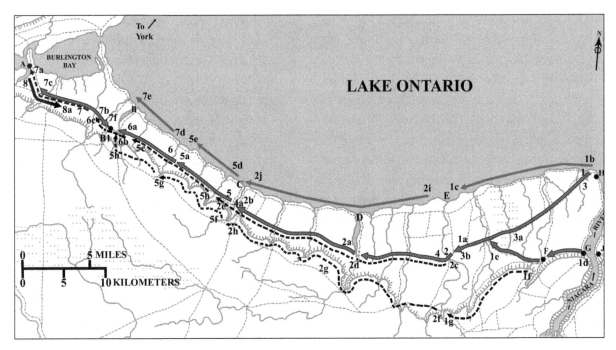

THE AMERICAN ADVANCE TO STONEY CREEK, JUNE 1–5, 1813

A   Burlington Heights
B   Stoney Creek
B1   Stoney Creek Battlefield
C   Forty Mile Creek
D   Twenty Mile Creek
E   Twelve Mile Creek
F   St. Davids
G   Queenston
H   Newark/Fort George
I   Fort Niagara
J   Lewiston

1. June 1
In pursuit of the retreating British Army, American forces, under Brigadier General Winder, march from Fort George following the Black Swamp trail (1,1a), while their supply boats move east along the lake (1b, 1c). At the same time, the Thirteenth Regiment, stationed at Queenston, marches to join the main column at Twelve Mile Creek (1d, 1e). On the escarpment, detachments of Canadian militia, supported by Native allies, begin to shadow and report on the American advance (1f, 1g).

2. June 2

The American force pushes forward (2, 2a, 2b), skirmishing with the British rearguard (Provincial Light Dragoons) and forcing it to retire (2c, 2d, 2e). The militias and Native allies on the escarpment maintain their surveillance (2f, 2g, 2h). Winder's united American force encamps at the Forty Mile Creek to await reinforcements, while their supply boats match the army's advance (2i, 2j).

3. June 3

A second American force, under Brigadier General Chandler (3), is dispatched in support of Winder's column and advances along the Black Swamp trail toward the Forty Mile Creek, reaching the Twelve Mile Creek on its first day's march (3a, 3b).

4. June 4–5

General Chandler's column continues its march toward the Forty, arriving around dawn on the 5th of June (4, 4a). The two forces are united under the overall command of General Chandler.

5. June 5, a.m.

The combined American force advances along the main road toward Burlington Heights (5, 5a), but is slowed in its advance by increased resistance from the cavalry rearguard (5b, 5c). Offshore, the American supply boats continue to move east (5d, 5e), while the Canadian militia and British Native allies on the hilltop move west to link up with the infantry rearguard at Stoney Creek (5f, 5g, 5h).

6. June 5, p.m.

The American advance continues into the afternoon (6, 6a) with the British infantry advance force (49th Regiment) (6b), augmented by the cavalry rearguard and units from the escarpment, make a fighting retreat (6c) that stalls the American advance.

7. Late in the afternoon, the Twenty-Fifth Regiment reinforces the American advance, forcing the British rearguard to retire to Burlington Heights (7, 7a), pressed by the Americans (7b, 7c). The main American army halts to the east of Stoney Creek and begins to encamp (B1), while their boats move up to the mouth of the creek (7d, 7e). The American advance force is recalled at sunset. (7f).

8. July 5–6

During the night, a British force marches from Burlington Heights to attack the American encampment (8, 8a).

guards; a move that was to have significant consequences later in the night.

Meanwhile, at Burlington Heights, General Vincent was facing the fact that as well as expecting an American attack, there were disturbing signs that American sympathizers had been fomenting dissent amongst the Native tribes. There was even the potential threat of a wholesale Native desertion to the American side in order to protect their lands and families from American aggression. Vincent also had to contend with the dilemma of either abandoning Burlington Heights, his main supply base and hub of land communications with Proctor, or taking the offensive against a superior enemy and risk the annihilation of his already depleted army. Instead, taking a gamble that he could stall the American advance long enough to

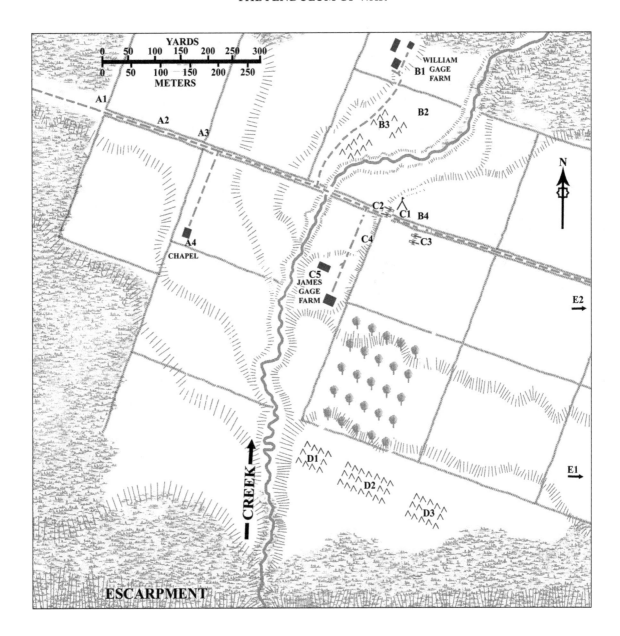

THE BATTLE OF STONEY CREEK, JUNE 5–6, 1813

Initial American Encampment positions

A1, A2, A3	Individual outlying American pickets along the road leading to Burlington Heights
A4	Left advanced picket post, U.S. Rifles
B1	Right advanced picket post, Twenty-Second Infantry
B2	Twenty-Third Regiment, Second Artillery Regiment
B3	(Initial position) Twenty-Fifth Regiment
B4	(Second position) Twenty-Fifth Regiment
C1	Command Tent, General Chandler, General Winder
C2	Artillery (Towson's) (unlimbered, in battery)
C3	Artillery (Leonard's) (limbered, in park)
C4	U.S Volunteers, First Rifles Regiment, Militia detachments (unspecified)
C5	Hill picket post, First Rifles Regiment, U.S. Volunteers, Militia detachments (unspecified)
D1	Fifth Regiment
D2	Sixteenth Regiment
D3	Twenty-Third Regiment
E1	(Off Map) Light Dragoons
E2	(Off Map) Ninth Regiment (rearguard)
E3	(Off Map) Thirteenth Regiment, Fourteenth Regiment, Second Artillery (Archer's) (at lakeside)

allow reinforcements to arrive, Vincent opted for a night attack on the American encampment. Accounts differ in their version of authorship for the assault. Certainly Vincent later credited Lieutenant Colonel Harvey (his deputy adjutant general) for the plan, but Harvey had not only received reconnaissance reports from his militia scouts, he had also made a personal reconnaissance of the American positions during the waning hours of daylight. There are also accounts of additional less-official intelligence sources. According to one story, Lieutenant James FitzGibbon (49th Regiment) was reputed to have dressed in woman's clothing and boldly entered the American camp, selling butter to the American troops while determining their positions before returning and giving a detailed account of the enemy weaknesses. Another tells of the contributions made by a local civilian youth Billy Green, who, in conjunction with his brother-in-law Isaac Corman, obtained the countersign to the American challenge for the night and reported it to Harvey.

Armed with this combined intelligence, Harvey sent Vincent a recommendation for a major attack, but was shocked when he received a reply rejecting the idea. Making a personal visit to Vincent, Harvey convinced his superior to reconsider his decision. Although he had a number of regular and militia regiments available, Vincent was still unwilling to

Above: A post-war view of the Stoney Creek battlefield, as seen from William Gage's farm and looking south toward the escarpment. The James Gage farmstead can be seen, centre mid-distant. The low ridge held by the Americans is to the left. The creek cutting through the field (where the Twenty-Fifth U.S. Infantry originally encamped) is in the centre foreground. The picket's chapel and graveyard is at the right far distant.

Right: The James Gage house as a museum in 2012, with top of the battlefield memorial monument showing behind and to the left.

risk everything on a single chance. Certain that this sortie could only delay the inevitable American advance, he limited the attack force to a total of five companies of regular troops from the 8th (King's) and the 49th Regiments.[2]

After initially placing Lieutenant Colonel Harvey in command, Vincent later decided to accompany the force in the role of observer. Reinforced on the march by a small band of Native warriors led by the still-loyal John Norton, and a detachment from the Light Company of the 49th Regiment, the British column moved through the darkness under strict orders to maintain absolute silence, which was ensured by not only keeping the muskets unloaded but also having the essential flints removed from the firing mechanisms, making the weapons little less than spears and clubs until they could be re-flinted (a procedure that this author can assure readers is a tricky job to do properly in daylight, while standing still, and with no pressure of time — but one that Vincent's troops would have to achieve in the dark, whilst engaged in an attack, and probably under enemy fire). Marching under an overhead blanket of low cloud and a light mist that helped to muffle any sound from carrying, the column arrived within striking range of the American encampment around 2:00 a.m. The Natives were then detached to take up flanking positions on the escarpment,

while the advance guard moved toward the flickering lights of the American campfires.

Although accounts vary about the exact sequence of events that followed, the most reliable sources concur that by using the acquired American passwords, the advance parties distracted the American pickets long enough to allow the raiders to quietly overpower two of the sentries and capture Captain Swearengen's sleeping advance guard in the chapel. Advancing further, the alarm was finally raised by another sentry, who was able to fire his musket before fleeing toward the American camp. The vital element of surprise was now lost and the main body of British troops surged forward. The 8th (King's) moved along the main road and to the right, directing their attack toward the James Gage farmstead, while the 49th moved to the left and charged into the tent lines of the absent Twenty-Fifth Regiment, bayoneting anyone they came across. Had this regiment remained in situ, it would undoubtedly have been overwhelmed and effectively annihilated, leaving a major breach in the American defensive line and opening the way for the British to attack the remaining disoriented American units piecemeal. Instead, the Americans were alerted to the attack that was approaching its relocated position. Thinking themselves already well into the American encampment and starting to receive fire, numbers of the British troops halted

ESTIMATE OF FORCES, BATTLE OF STONEY CREEK, JUNE 6, 1813[2]

British

(Brigadier General Vincent)
8th (King's) Regiment (Major Ogilvie), 280 all ranks
49th Regiment (Major Plenderleath), 430 all ranks
Royal Artillery (Lieutenant Richard Armstrong), 1 gun, est.15–20 all ranks
Lincoln and York Embodied Militias (unknown commander), est. 25–40 all ranks
Native Allies (John Norton), British estimates 20–60 warriors, Native oral accounts 150–200 warriors
Estimated Total Force: 800–900 all ranks

American

Right Wing (Brigadier General Chandler)
Light Troops (detached from the Second Artillery) (Captain Biddle/Captain Hindman/Captain Nicholas), est.150 all ranks
First Rifle Regiment (Captain Van Swearingen), est. 20 all ranks
Twenty-Second Regiment (Captain Daniel McFarland/Captain Milliken), est.120 all ranks (stationed at the Methodist church)
Twenty-Fifth Regiment (Major Joseph Smith), est. 675 all ranks

Centre
Second Artillery (Captain Towson/Lieutenant Leonard), 8 guns and crews, est.100 all ranks

Captain Thomas Biddle (Not engaged as artillery in the battle, fought as infantry), est. 200 all ranks

Left Wing (Brigadier General Winder)
Fifth/Twentieth Regiment (Lieutenant Colonel H. Milton), est. 300 all ranks
Sixteenth Regiment (Colonel Pearce), est. 300 all ranks
Twenty-Third Regiment (Major Henry Armstrong), est. 400 all ranks
First Rifle Regiment (Major Forsyth), est. 60 all ranks
Volunteer Riflemen (Captain John Lyttle), est. 55 all ranks

Rear Guard
Second Light Dragoon Regiment (Colonel James Burn), est.175 all ranks
Ninth Regiment (Captain George Bender), est.120 All ranks

Lakeside (Lieutenant Colonel Chrystie), not engaged in the action
Thirteenth Regiment (Major Huyck), est. 450 all ranks
Fourteenth Regiment (Lieutenant Colonel Charles Boerstler), est. 380 all ranks
Artillery (Captain Archer), est. 50 all ranks
Boat Crews (unknown commander), est. 200 all ranks

Estimated Total Force (including staff and non-combatant support): 3,550 all ranks

and used the illumination of the American camp-fires to install their flints, load their own weapons, and return fire upon the unseen enemy. Because of this, as it was still outside of the American main line, silhouetted against the light of the fires and fully exposed to the view of the Americans, the disorganized British advance stalled. Even then, a steady command to form line could have maintained the upper hand for the British and restored the impetus of the attack. Instead, some of the officers of Vincent's staff began cheering and whooping in the manner of the Natives, either thinking that a complete victory was already achieved or attempting to create the impression that this was a Native attack and using the calls to instill additional fear and confusion in their enemy. With the example of their officers sounding in their ears, the rank and file took up the cheers and yells. As a result, effective control of the still forming British battle line collapsed. Certain officers, like FitzGibbon, restrained their men and began to pour a steady destructive fire into the Americans forming on the rising ground ahead. Other segments of the British force, however, impulsively pressed forward unsupported and engaged in a melee of hand-to-hand combat with their enemy. According to one unidentified American officer, "The horses of the cavalry and infantry bursting in amongst us at every direction. General Chandler running about crying, 'Where is the Line? Where is the Line' General Winder in the same manner exclaiming 'Come on'.... No orders passing from or to any Corps or officer. May my eyes never witness such a scene again."[3]

Things were not any better on the British side of the engagement, according to Lieutenant FitzGibbon. "Our men never ceased shouting. No order could be heard. Everything was noise and confusion.... Our men returned fire contrary to orders and it soon became apparent that it was impossible to prevent shouting and firing."[4]

Without any proper command and control, the battle degenerated into combat between individual companies and sections, aiming at shapes seen by the light of musket flashes and campfires. Inevitably casualties to "friendly fire" occurred.

Towson with his field pieces was stationed in the road and was pouring a destructive fire of grape and canister through the dark upon the British ... when he was ordered by Genl. Winder to change the direction of his fire ... upon a meadow where the advance were warmly engaged with the British.... Thus the advance of the American army was placed between two most galling and destructive fires, Vincent with his British column in front and the grape and canister from Towson's

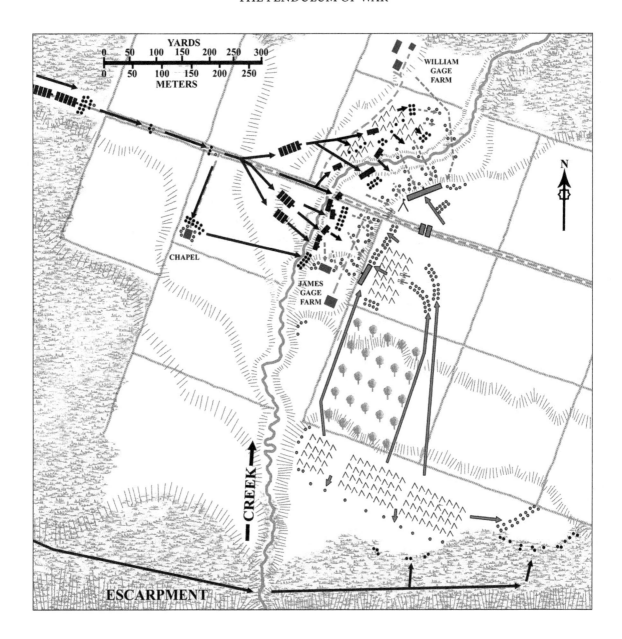

THE BATTLE OF STONEY CREEK, JUNE 5–6, 1813

Initial British Attack and American Response.

1. The British column (1) advances upon the American position, moving down the road leading from Burlington Heights, while a detachment of Native Allies move round on the south flank along the slope of the escarpment (1a, 1b). The British advance guard eliminates the two initial American picket sentries (A1, A2) without causing any alarm, but the third (A3) resists and is either captured or bayonetted.

2. The leading element of the British force rushes south and overwhelms the American picket post (A4) at the Methodist chapel (2). An additional American sentry (location unspecified), hearing noises in the darkness, fires his musket as an alarm to alert the American camp. The main body of the British column now advances at a run, with the companies of the 8th (King's) Regiment moving to the right of the road (2a), while the companies of the 49th Regiment move left and rush the partially occupied tented encampment of the Twenty-Fifth Regiment (2b) causing those troops still in that location to flee toward the American main line (2c).

3. Responding to the alarm, the American advance guard at William Gage's farm. Nearby U.S. units (B1, B2) find themselves almost cut off and engage in a running fight with the advancing British troops as they attempt to make their way back to the American positions on the other side of the creek (3, 3a, 3b), only to come under friendly fire from the main American line. The main body of the Twenty-Fifth Regiment (B4), previously relocated to the rising ground beside Towson's artillery battery (C2), move forward and form line along the top of the embankment, securing the American right flank (3c).

4. American units encamped around the James Gage farmstead (C4, C5) also rush to their rallying positions around the farm and along the fence line marking the slight rise of ground to the east of the farm (4, 4a, 4b).

5. On the high ground, at the foot of the escarpment, the bulk of the American units who had encamped there (Fifth [D1], Sixteenth [D2], and Twenty-Third [D3] regiments) move down the hill to join the American positions directly under attack (5, 5a, 5b, 5c, 5d, 5e), while their picket sentries and remaining detachments (5f, 5g, 5h) seek to secure their encampment from the harassing fire from the British Native Allies (5i, 5j).

6. As American resistance stiffens and the British troops need to reflint their muskets, the British advance stalls. As a result, in the darkness a disorganized line of battle, composed of individual companies and sections, is established (6, 6a, 6b, 6c).

pieces in the rear and upon the left flank. Such was the difficulty of extricating in any way the advance, that after having many killed and wounded by the grape and canister of Towson's pieces, they were obliged to break and almost singly fall back upon their own army.[5]

— Lieutenant Johnathan Kearsley,
Second U.S. Artillery

Kearsley himself was nearly captured as he sought to assess the position of the units to his left

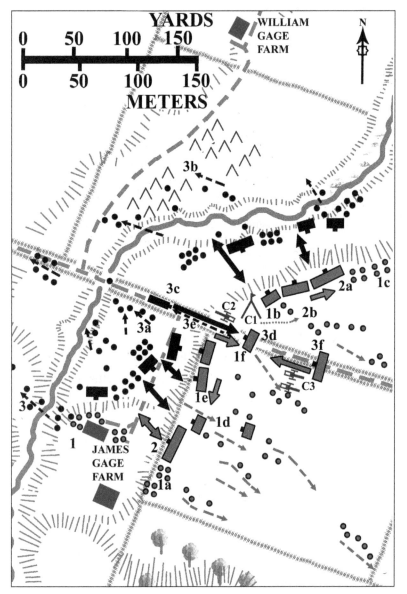

BATTLE OF STONEY CREEK

The Capture of the American Guns

1. In the confusion of the darkness, the battle degenerates into series of independent engagements at almost point-blank range, that fluctuate across the ground below the rise marking the American front line (1, 1a, 1b, 1c). At the centre of the American line, the Sixteenth Regiment is partially broken and routs, leaving a gap (1d), while the Twenty-Third is forced to extend its front to both the left to cover the gap (1e) and right to support the guns (1f). Towson's artillery (C2) is a particular threat to the British as it continues to fire.

2. Hearing additional firing on their flanks, the American commanders order the Fifth (2) on the left, and Twenty-Fifth (2a) on the right, to redeploy and extend their lines. General Chandler moves from his command position (C1) toward the right flank and is thrown from his horse (2b).

3. Within the British line unit cohesion is crumbling, as individuals and groups of men look to retire from the close-quarter action (3, 3a, 3b). Near the centre, Major Plenderleath (49th Regiment) leads a desperate charge on Towson's

battery (3c, C2). Overrunning the guns, his detachment presses forward and routs a detachment of the Twenty-Third Regiment (3d). Generals Chandler and Winder, plus a significant number of officers and men, are subsequently captured and removed to the rear, while Plenderleath's men begin to haul off two of the American guns (3e). Hearing this noise, a detachment from the Sixteenth Regiment (3f) advances and counterattacks, pushing the British out from the artillery position and securing the remainder of the guns of Towson's battery (3f, C2).

4. The battle winds down as both sides suffer increasing amounts of attrition of manpower from the losses in killed and wounded, as well as individuals and groups of men breaking off from the action and moving to the rear of their respective front lines. As a result, the two forces become separated and the fighting concludes with both sides retreating.

and walked right up to a line of troops in the darkness. Upon being challenged by the officer of the line in front of him in a thick Irish brogue, Kearsley realized that these were not his own but British troops, and tried to talk his way out of his predicament by identifying himself as a "friend"; but his accent as an American was seemingly as distinctive as the Irishman who challenged him, and under a fusillade of answering shots he was forced to scurry off into the darkness. To the credit of the Americans, although some units broke and ran toward the tree-covered escarpment for cover (only to find themselves fired on from the slopes by the Natives stationed there),

others soon recovered and began to fire with such determination that the Canadian militia officer, Captain W. H. Merritt, later recorded: "Colonel Harvey and the officers were using every exertion to get the men formed when the enemy opened a most tremendous fire on us from the Hill, likewise opened their guns.... I never heard so rapid a discharge of Musquetry, the hill was a Continual sheet of fire. Our men were dispersed in every direction.[6]

Unable to breach the ever-strengthening American positions along the small ridge, increasing numbers of the already disorganized British line began to retire.

> The officers could no longer control their men and soon began to fall back. The company I commanded, up to this moment, was kept in good order ... but when I saw the men falling back and no field officer near, I ran along the line to the left to prevent the men retreating, although I was almost convinced that their remaining under the enemy's fire could be of no use. Yet I had some hopes that good order might be restored.[7]
>
> — Lieutenant James FitzGibbon, 49th Regiment

At this moment, when the whole British line was in danger of collapse, the American commanders heard the sounds of firing upon both their left and right flanks. Supposing this to be an attempt by the British to outflank the American line, detachments of the Fifth Regiment on the left and Twenty-Fifth on the right were ordered to relocate and extend in either direction to secure the supposedly threatened ground, while the Twenty-Third Regiment was left to maintain the centre of the line and support the artillery in front. In fact, General Chandler was sufficiently concerned that he rode off into the darkness toward the right flank, only to have his horse fall, throwing him heavily to the ground and knocking him unconscious at what was to be the crisis of the battle.

The cenotaph cairn at Stoney Creek, located near to the position originally occupied by the American artillery battery that was charged and captured by the British.

Back in the British line, Major Plenderleath (49th Regiment), far from retreating, led a party of men in a charge toward Towson's guns that reached the battery relatively intact, whereupon the British soldiers wasted no time in bayoneting and shooting the surprised artillerymen before pressing forward to engage a detachment of the Twenty-Third Regiment stationed behind the guns. Despite being significantly superior in numbers, the Americans were totally unprepared to receive this assault and were only able to fire a single volley before breaking under the British onslaught. Securing the guns, the British added to their score of cannons and crew when a revived General Chandler suddenly walked out of the darkness and right into the middle of the artillery position. He began to physically manhandle some of the British soldiers, exhorting them to recommence firing the cannon — as he obviously thought in the darkness of the night and concussion of his fall that he was addressing his own artillerymen. Quickly disabused of this error, Chandler was thus captured and placed under guard. As if this coup was not enough, only moments later it was topped off by the similar capture of General Winder. With only a few dozen men, Plenderleath sensibly did not push his luck too far, and with his "bag" of two generals, several senior field officers, and nearly one hundred other ranks, ordered his men to retire after spiking the guns that could not be brought off. Using captured horses to drag off two of the American artillery pieces, the British began their retreat. This action, however, attracted the attention of the Sixteenth Regiment, who were stationed further back on the road. In response, a detachment of men under Lieutenant McChesney made a counterattack upon the retiring British and secured the remaining guns of the battery from being taken as well.

Only an hour had passed since the first shot rang out across the battlefield, but having suffered over 200 casualties, nearly 30 percent of his force, Lieutenant Colonel Harvey was concerned about revealing his numerical inferiority with the approaching dawn. He therefore ordered a general withdrawal, convinced he had suffered a tactical defeat. In addition, Brigadier General Vincent, who had been stationed on the British left flank, had disappeared and was now feared killed or captured. With no one to report to, Harvey withdrew to Burlington Heights to await an expected American assault within the next few days.

Unbeknownst to Harvey, confusion also reigned in the American camp. The army had lost its two commanding generals, as well as other senior officers, leaving individual captains and subalterns wandering around in the darkness, attempting to reform their scattered troops. Without effective leadership, individual detachments began to withdraw east,

some only a few hundred yards, others upwards of a mile, leaving behind their dead and wounded, and abandoning anything that could not be immediately carried away. In the gray light of dawn, command of the American army initially fell on a relatively junior officer, Colonel James Burn (Second Light Dragoons). Uncertain as to how to proceed, he called a council of officers to elicit their views.

After considerable debate on the question of who held the senior commission and therefore commanded the remaining forces, it was found, much to the disappointment of the more aggressive Colonel Chrystie (Thirteenth Regiment), that Burns had seniority. Not having been involved in the night's action (as he and his regimental command were stationed at the lakefront to guard the boats and secure the main road), Chrystie still wanted to continue the advance. Opposing this, the more cautious Burn cited the night's casualties, the current disorder of the remaining regiments, and the losses in ammunition and supplies as strong reasons to retire and regroup. After an acrimonious exchange of views amongst the command officers, Burn later recorded: "A majority coincided in opinion with me that we ought to retire to our former position at the Forty Mile Creek, where we could be supplied with ammunition and provisions and either advance or remain until further orders."[8]

The battlefield memorial monument, built to commemorate the hundredth anniversary of the battle.

OFFICIAL CASUALTIES, BATTLE OF STONEY CREEK, JUNE 6, 1813[9]

British

Killed:	1 officer, 22 other ranks
Wounded:	12 officers, 2 drummers, 122 other ranks
Missing/Prisoners:	55 other ranks

(N.B. American accounts refer to British losses of 60 rank and file dead and captured from the 49th Regiment alone, while the British account for this regiment admits to losing only 39 rank and file.)

Native Allies (Native accounts)

Killed: 6 warriors

American

Killed:	17 other ranks
Wounded:	1 officer, 37 other ranks
Prisoners:	2 brigadier generals, 7 officers, 116 other ranks

(N.B. British accounts refer to burying over 50 bodies, while prisoner-of-war registers at Quebec City list 2 brigadier generals, 5 officers, 1 sergeant major, 2 musicians, 124 other ranks, 3 servants, and a 10-year-old boy being taken prisoner during this engagement.)

Meanwhile, Chrystie's two untouched regiments, the Thirteenth and Fourteenth, moved up onto the battlefield. However, they only stayed long enough to carry off the wounded and scavenge what they could of the abandoned American supplies before setting fire to whatever remained and retiring under the threat of increased numbers of Natives and Canadian militia appearing along the escarpment.

Back at Burlington, Harvey was relieved to see Brigadier General Vincent return to camp, albeit without his horse, hat, and sword. According to various accounts, he had either been found wandering around in the woods by Native warriors, a party of militia, or had hidden in the woods before walking alone back into the British camp. Embarrassed at getting separated from his horse and men while the battle raged on without him, he did bring the positive news that the Americans were retreating. Despite this, Vincent decided that the night's losses had left him without the resources to pursue the enemy in any effective manner. He therefore retained his defensive position with his regulars at Burlington, while ordering two companies of the Incorporated Militia, supported by Native warriors, to return to the escarpment and report on any subsequent American movements.[*9]

CHAPTER 7

The Pendulum Swings Back

Late in the afternoon of June 6th, reports of the battle at Stoney Creek reached General Dearborn at Fort George. In response, he ordered Major General Lewis to advance and take overall command of the American forces. He also attached the commands of Brigadier Generals Boyd and Swartout and Colonel Winfield Scott to ensure the offensive was maintained. However, Lewis delayed his departure overnight, as it was raining and according to Brigadier General Peter B. Porter's later description:

> ... he could not go sixteen miles to fight the enemy, not because his force was too small, but because he had not wagons to carry tents and camp kettles for his army. His own baggage moves in two stately wagons ... carrying the various furniture of a Secretary of State's Office, a lady's dressing chamber, an alderman's dining room, and the contents of a grocer's shop.[1]

THE SKIRMISH AT FORTY MILE CREEK, JUNE 8, 1813

Shortly after Lewis' departure on the morning of June 7th, an alarmed Dearborn sent a recall order, as a fleet of ships had been sighted sailing westerly toward the Head-of-the-Lake, and Dearborn was afraid (justifiably as it turned out) that these were British vessels transporting reinforcements for Vincent. However, less than two hours later he sent a countermanding order stating: "It is possible the fleet in sight may be our own, a few hours will probably enable you to determine and act accordingly."[2] Receiving these contradictory orders while on the march, Lewis simply continued on and reached the American encampment at Forty Mile Creek at around 5:00 p.m. To his concern, Lewis saw that the dominant escarpment was occupied by enemy troops and Natives, who were now openly showing themselves to intimidate Burn's already shaken command. In addition, just before dusk, the British naval vessels appeared offshore. In his subsequent report to Secretary of War Armstrong, Lewis recorded:

> At dawn of day [the 8th] we struck our Tents, and descried the Hostile Squadron abreast of us about a mile from the shore. Our boats, which transported the principal part of our Baggage and Camp Equipage lay on the Beach, it was a dead calm; at about six, the enemy towed in a large Schooner which opened her fire on our Boats. As soon as she stood for the shore, her object being evident, I ordered down Archer's and Towson's Companies with four pieces of artillery to resist her attempts…. Her fire was returned with a vivacity and effect … which soon compelled her to retire. A party of savages now made their appearance on the Brow of the mountain (which being perfectly bald, exhibited them to view) and commenced a fire on our Camp. I ordered Col. Christie [Chrystie] to dislodge them … but found himself anticipated by Lieut. Eldridge, the Adjutant of his Regiment, who … had already gained the summit of the mountain and with a party of volunteers had routed some militia and the Barbarian allies of the defender of the Christian faith.[3]

From the point of view of the aforementioned militia, the events of the previous two days were seen somewhat differently. Watching from their vantage point of the top of the escarpment during the course of June 6, 1813, two companies from the Incorporated Militia (Captain James Kerby and Captain Abraham Rapelje), supported by a small detachment of Native allies, could clearly assess the strength of the American force spread out along the Forty Mile Creek on the plain below. They also saw beyond, out on Lake Ontario, the welcome sight of Yeo's flotilla sailing west, with decks visibly crowded with red-coated troops. Consequently, it was fully expected that with this additional support Vincent would soon make his counterattack. However, by the

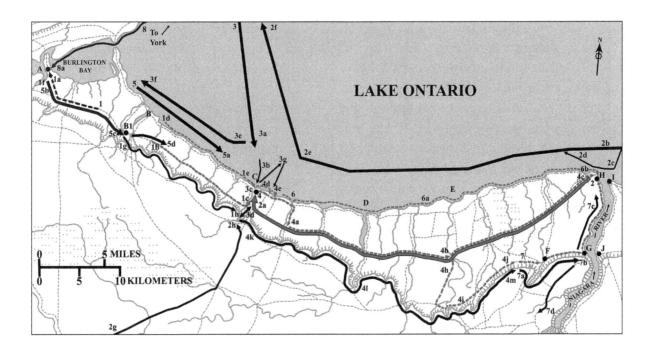

1. June 6

Immediately following the battle, British forces retreat from Stoney Creek (B1) to Burlington Heights (A) (1, 1a), while the American forces retreat to Forty Mile Creek (C) during the morning (1b, 1c). The American flotilla of supply boats also retreat to the Forty (1d, 1e). In the afternoon, detachments of Incorporated Militia of Upper Canada and Native allies are sent as an advance reconnaissance force from Burlington Heights to the escarpment to watch the Americans (1f, 1g 1h).

2. June 7

U.S. General Lewis' column advances from Fort George early in the morning (2), arriving at the Forty around 5:00 p.m. (2a). During the morning Commodore Yeo's fleet passes the Niagara River (2b), with two vessels breaking off to make a detailed inshore reconnaissance (2c, 2d) before rejoining the fleet. Yeo continues west, arriving off the Forty Mile Creek (2e) before sailing toward York (2f). On the escarpment the Incorporated Militia detachments and Native allies continue their reconnaissance (1h), while additional groups of Native reinforcements begin to arrive in significant numbers (2g, 2h).

3. June 8, a.m.

Yeo's squadron sails from York (3), and closes on the American encampment shortly after dawn (3a). Two ships from the squadron (*Beresford* and *Sir Sydney Smith*) are detached with orders to draw inshore and fire on the American encampment (3b), which is

130

returned with counter battery fire from the U.S. artillery (3c). On the escarpment the Natives engage in a sortie against the American encampment (3d) but are driven off, leading to the small exchange of fire between American detachments and the Incorporated Militia on the heights of the escarpment (1h).

Following the ineffective exchange of artillery fire, the bulk of Yeo's squadron sails west to land their infantry reinforcements (3e, 3f), while the *Beresford* and *Sir Sydney Smith* take up station father offshore (3g) to maintain a surveillance of the Americans.

4. June 8, a.m to p.m

Receiving urgent orders from General Dearborn to make an immediate retreat, General Lewis abandons his camp at the Forty Mile Creek. The initial column of American troops leave later in the morning and march directly back to Fort George (4, 4a, 4b, 4c). The American supply boats sail (4d), but are subsequently intercepted by the offshore British boats (4e). At least twelve American boats are captured or are driven ashore by their crews and abandoned. General Lewis begins his own retreat before noon, initially taking the same route as the previous column (4, 4a 4b), but then diverts and takes a circuitous route along the foot of the escarpment (4h, 4i, 4j). During this retreat, he is shadowed on the heights by the Incorporated Militia and Native allies, which are further reinforced, while on the march, with a detachment from the 49th Regiment (Lieutenant Fitzgibbon) (4k, 4l, 4m).

5. June 8, p.m.

At Burlington Heights the news of the American retreat causes General Vincent to send Yeo back to the Forty Mile Creek with the reinforcements (5, 5a), where they land and occupy the abandoned American position. General Lewis also begins a land advance (5b, 5c) spearheaded by detachments from the 41st and 49th Regiments (5d), who press on to the Forty by nightfall.

6. Evading capture, the remaining American boats (6) continue on toward the Niagara River (6a), only to be fired on by their own troops in the darkness (6b).

7. June 9

The American column of General Lewis (7), continues its retreat via St. Davids (F), Queenston (G) to Fort George (H), arriving there around 9:00 p.m. The shadowing force, under the command of Lieutenant Fitzgibbon (7a), arrives on the heights above Queenston (7b) and divides, with part continuing to trail the Americans (7c) while other detachments move south to secure Chippawa and extend their reconnaissance toward Fort Erie (7d).

8. A flotilla of Native warriors from Lower Canada (8) arrive in canoes to reinforce the British positions on the Niagara (8a).

B	Stoney Creek
D	Twenty Mile Creek
E	Twelve Mile Creek
I	Fort Niagara
J	Lewiston

following morning, Vincent had still not made an appearance. Instead, additional Native forces began to appear as news of the British success emboldened those who had previously been conspicuous by their absence. Later in the day, movement of a strong column was seen on the plain below, not coming from the west as hoped but rather from the direction of Fort George in the east, as Major

General Lewis arrived to bolster the American position. The opportunity for a quick British victory had been lost and, after sending back messengers to Burlington, the men of the Incorporated Militia could only watch and wait for Vincent's orders.

On the 8th, as Yeo's ships fired on the American camp, the Native troops were clamouring to descend the escarpment and make an attack from the rear upon the Americans while their focus was on the ongoing action at the lake. Under orders to maintain his reconnaissance duties and not to unnecessarily hazard his men, Kerby declined to attack but, seeing the Natives were determined, sent Rapelje's company down the slope in support, while he remained

This modern view, looking northeast toward the Niagara River from the strategically dominant top of the escarpment at Forty Mile Creek (Grimsby), clearly shows how this vantage point allowed the Incorporated Militia and their Native allies to report on every move the Americans made during their advance and subsequent retreat from Stoney Creek.

in a position to see how matters developed and moved as required. As expected, the initial Native foray succeeded in penetrating the southern fringe of the camp. However, the Americans soon rallied and counterattacked, sending the Natives running for the escarpment, hotly pursued by Lieutenant Eldridge's men. As a result, Rapelje's company was forced to make a fighting retreat to cover the rout of the Natives. Pressed back up the slope, Rapelje's men slowed the American advance until the crest of the escarpment was reached, whereupon Kerby's line awaited the advancing Americans. Forming on Kerby's flank, the two companies of Incorporated Militia brought Eldridge's men to a complete

A modern view (2012) of the narrow stretch of land that separates the escarpment from Lake Ontario. This was the location of the skirmish at the Forty Mile Creek on June 8, 1813.

halt with a single disciplined volley of musketry. Disorganized and blown, the Americans threw back a few shots and then retired back down the slopes to their camp, leaving the militiamen to resume their watch of the American camp.

During this same period, seeking to secure his seeming advantage, Sir James Yeo attempted to pressure the Americans into surrender, as Lewis also recorded.

> Sir James Yeo ... next determined in true Dramatic Style, to amuse us with a farce. An Officer with a flag was sent to me from his Ship advising me that as I was invested with Savages in my rear, a fleet in my front, & a powerful army on my flank, he, and the officers commanding his Brittanick Majesty's land forces, thought it their duty to demand a surrender of My army. I answered that the message was too Ridiculous to merit a reply.[4]

Seemingly confident in his position, supported by aggressive subordinates and with a substantial force under his command, Lewis could have continued the American campaign simply by maintaining his position. However, back at Fort George, Dearborn had become increasingly agitated about his divided forces and on the afternoon of the 7th penned a further urgent order (No. 7) to Lewis that was received by Lewis the following morning.

> I am induced to suspect that the Enemy's fleet have an intention on this place, two small Schooners have been examining the shore very minutely for three or four hours this afternoon. They have gone on toward the Head of the Lake, and their Ships appear to have taken the same Course. They may take on board additional Troops near the Head of the Lake and be here before you reach this place. You will please to send Milton's detachment [Fifth Regiment] & 500 of Chandler's Brigade and Col. Burn's Light Dragoons with all possible dispatch.... You will follow with the remainder of the troops as soon as practicable, it will be necessary to take care that your boats are not taken or lost. Genl. Swartout and Col. Scott should return as soon as they can....

> H. Dearborn[5]

Stripped of his aggressive commanders, a substantial part of his army, and under direct orders to return to Fort George, Lewis had no option but to abandon the offensive. However, after dispatching the required units to march back to Fort George post haste and ordering the supply boats to sail along the shoreline in concert, he became so concerned that his retreat would be cut off by troops landed from Yeo's fleet that, instead of following Milton and Chandler's brigade on the most direct route back to the mouth of the river, he marched his remaining troops inland and took a circuitous route by way of Twelve Mile Creek, St. Davids, and Queenston — further dividing his force and, in fact, increasing the threat of their capture if the British had, indeed, been following the Americans more closely. After finally arriving at Fort George late in the evening of June 9th and assuming the command of the American forces around Fort George, due to the "temporary indisposition of Major General Dearborn,"[6] Lewis submitted a highly critical report to his brother-in-law, secretary of war, Armstrong, in which he:

- Blamed General Chandler for the defeat at Stoney Creek:

> … a view of Chandler's encampment will be sufficient to show that this disaster was owing to its Injudicious arrangement. Its centre being its weakest point and that being discovered by the enemy in the evening,

received the combined attack of his whole force, and his line was completely cut: (It is said, though I cannot vouch for its truth, that Winder saw this and remonstrated against it).[7]

- Undermined Dearborn's authority by quoting his commander's vacillating orders as "proof" of his unfitness to command, and claiming that the American force was rapidly deteriorating in fighting efficiency due to his failure in leadership:

> … our Army is dwindling away from fatigue Nakedness and disease … the fine army of 4450 men with which I landed on this shore, though increased by the junction of Preston's Regiment, has dwindled down to about three thousand effectives…. The Enemy's fleet is constantly hovering on our Coast and interrupting our supplies.[8]

- Painted the retreat from the Forty Mile Creek, under his command, as being undertaken with discipline and only a minor degree of accidental loss and enemy pressure:

No. 7 was delivered to me about 6 this morning [June 8th]. Between 7 and 8 oclk the few wagons we had being loaded, first with sick and next with ammunition etc. the residue of Camp Equipage & Baggage was put in the Boats, and a detachment of two Hundred Men of the Sixth Regiment detailed to proceed in them — Orders were prepared to be given them to defend the Boats, and if assailed by any of the Enemy's small vessels to carry them by Boarding. By some irregularity, which I have not been able to discover, the Boats put off without the detachments, induced probably by the Stillness of the morning. When they had progressed about 3 miles, a Breeze Sprang up and an armed Schooner overhauled them; those who were enterprising kept on and escaped. Others ran to the Shore and deserted their Boats. We lost twelve of the numbers, principally containing the Baggage of the Officers and Men. At ten I put the Army in motion on our return to this place [Fort George], The Savages, and Incorporated Militia hung on our

flanks and rear throughout the march and picked up a few straglers.[9]

The reality was that by the time Lewis arrived at Fort George the American losses had accumulated to:

— 200–300 men killed, wounded or missing at Stoney Creek and the Forty Mile Creek.
— 80 "straglers" captured in the retreat
— 2 artillery pieces
— 500 tents
— 100 muskets
— 140 barrels of flour
— 10 barrels of pork
— 200 Camp kettles
— 1 Commissariat wagon
— 1 Medicine Chest
— 16- 20 bateaux and boats and the baggage they carried.[10]

As if to enhance the magnitude of the failure of the American campaign, those boats that had avoided capture did not escape unscathed, as that night they were fired upon by Dearborn's troops as they approached the Niagara River, suffering several additional casualties from the friendly fire. For all intents, the American invasion campaign had collapsed and the previously victorious army of York and Fort George had been precipitously herded back to their landing grounds by an inferior number of (but greatly more aggressive) militia and Native warriors — backed by British regulars and naval units.

Similarly seeking to avoid censure, General Dearborn's official report to Armstrong deliberately underrated the American casualty figures and overestimated those of the enemy troops engaged at Stoney Creek. He also played up the valour of his troops and even went so far as to claim that, in his judgement, Stoney Creek was a decisive victory for the Americans, compromised only by the unfortunate loss of their two generals.

As might be expected, the repercussions of the collapse of the American offensive were not long in coming — but contained some surprises. Although General Dearborn had already submitted his letter of resignation on June 14th (upon the grounds he was sick and incapable of carrying out his duties), he was retained as senior commander; while General Lewis, who had worked so hard to avoid blame and fully expected to have made permanent his temporary elevation to senior commander, found himself reassigned to Sackets Harbor and replaced by Brigadier General Boyd. After consulting with Dearborn, Boyd placed the American army entirely on the defensive by ordering the garrisons at Fort Erie, Chippawa, and Queenston to

destroy their positions and retire to Fort George. There, extensive efforts were made to complete the reconstruction of the reduced perimeter of fortifications, while to the north additional defence lines were constructed between the fort and the town to create a fortified enclave that became the main American camp. Finally, as a contingency in case of a future setback, boats were gathered below the fort to execute any potential evacuation orders.

For the British, Yeo's arrival had brought badly needed reinforcements that included detachments from the 8th (King's), 104th, and Royal Newfoundland Regiments, as well as supplies for what was termed the "Centre Division." As a result, there was an opportunity to make a dynamic counteroffensive to retake the frontier. However, constrained by Prevost's entirely defence-minded policies, after advancing and occupying the American camp at the Forty on the afternoon of the 8th, Vincent made only a slow and cautious advance toward the American position at Newark. On the other hand, the enhanced detachments of Native allies, the two companies of Incorporated Militia, and a detachment of the 49th Regiment (Lieutenant James FitzGibbon), who were independently advancing on the army's southern flank above the escarpment, took the opportunity to press ahead and reclaim the remainder of the Niagara frontier for British control. Vincent also received additional reinforcements in the form of over 300 volunteer Native warriors, drawn from the Seven Nations of Lower Canada. These men had completed a journey of some 500 miles (800 kilometers) in canoes that led them from their homes near Montreal, up against the current of the St. Lawrence River to Kingston, and then following the shoreline of Lake Ontario past York and Burlington Heights to the fighting on the Niagara.

This American reversal of fortune also impacted strongly on the Upper Canada civilian populace as it solidified the rift between that segment of the population that had supported the American cause and those who were loyal to the Crown. Having openly hailed the earlier American invasion and victories, the current state of defeat and retreat exposed these American sympathizers to reprisals for being traitors. In response, many fled into the United States, while others, led by a prominent former member of the Upper Canada Legislature, Joseph Willcocks, sought protection by forming a military corps of "Canadian Volunteers" and offered their services to the American commander. During the forthcoming months, these turncoats used their local knowledge to good advantage for the American cause in the form of scouting and gathering intelligence. But they also abused their place in the U.S. military system by taking out their own personal grudges against their former neighbours and political opponents under the excuse of wartime necessity. The result was an increasing level of resentment and active opposition from the local civilians, creating a sub-conflict of violence that would only escalate over the coming months.

CHAPTER 8

The Warning Must Be Given: The Battle of Beaver Dams, June 24, 1813

By mid-June 1813, the American-occupied invasion zone in Upper Canada consisted of a self-imposed perimeter of only a couple of square miles around the town of Newark. Inside this area, a force of over 6,000 American troops were bottled up by a combined force of around 3,000 British regulars, Canadian militia, and British Native allies, whose constricting front ran in a line from Lake Ontario to the Niagara escarpment, roughly paralleling the course of the Four Mile Creek. In particular, the augmented forces of the British Native allies were aggressive in sniping at and ambushing the American outlying pickets. At dawn on June 23rd one detachment, under the command of Dominique Ducharme, went so far as to infiltrate behind the American left flank and reached the Niagara River, where they ambushed a large boat filled with American troops bringing supplies downriver from Lewiston. Killing four and capturing seven of the crew, they were only prevented in taking off the boat's supplies by the arrival of a detachment of American Dragoons, who forced the warriors to retire to the cover of the nearby woods with the loss of only one individual, who rashly attempted to capture a horse as a trophy. Responding to these incursions, Brigadier General Boyd decided that a simultaneous, bold counter strike against two of the British outposts was required. However, while the nearest British force was only two miles away at the "Crossroads" (present-day Virgil), and was initially included as a target, no attack on this post was attempted. Instead, the only expedition that took place was commanded by Lieutenant Colonel Charles Boerstler

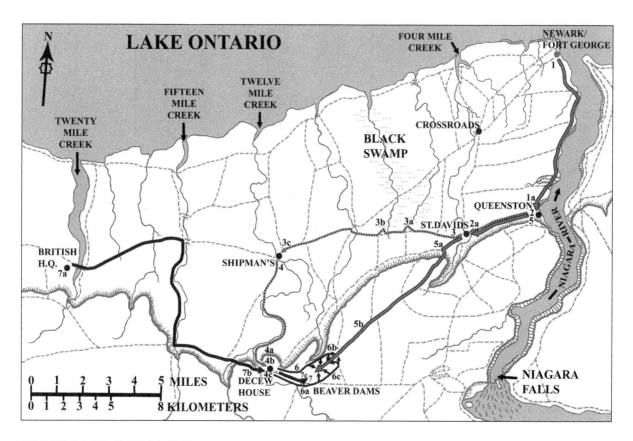

BEAVER DAMS, JUNE 24, 1813

1. The American force (under Lieutenant Colonel Boerstler) marches from Fort George (1) to Queenston (1a) and occupies buildings within the village.

2. Learning of the American plan to attack the DeCew house and Fitzgibbon's troops, Laura Secord leaves her home (2) to give warning. She evades Boerstler's pickets and reaches the home of her brother at St. Davids (2a).

3. Laura Secord leaves St. Davids and, in order to avoid American patrols and possible road blocks on a direct route to DeCew's, is forced to take a wide diversionary route following the road and cutting across country (3, 3a), including the southern fringe of the Black Swamp (3b), and reaches Shipman's Corners (St. Catharines) (3c).

4. Leaving Shipman's Corners (4), Laura Secord enters the dense bush, following the line of the Twelve Mile

Creek until she reaches the escarpment (4a). Scaling the escarpment, an exhausted Laura Secord comes across an encampment of Natives in a field near DeCew's (4b). She is taken to Fitzgibbon and warns him of Boerstler's advance (4c).

5. The Americans advance from Queenston (5) to St. Davids, ascend the escarpment (5a), and move on Beaver Dams (5b).

6. British-Native allies advance (6, 6a) and attack Boerstler's column from the rear and flanks (6b, 6c) while it is marching through restricted terrain.

7. Fitzgibbon's force advances on Beaver Dams (7) and stalls for time to allow Major DeHaren's column march from its encampment at Twenty Mile Creek (7a) to the battlefield (7b, 7c).

Toronto Reference Library, JRR 1343.

Above: *The DeCou House*, J.W. Cotton, artist, circa 1913. A view of the DeCew or De Cou house before it was destroyed by a suspicious fire in 1950.

Below: The preserved foundations of the DeCew house are all that remain of the property in 2012.

AMERICAN FORCE,
BATTLE OF BEAVER DAMS, JUNE 24, 1813[1]

(Lieutenant Colonel Boerstler)
Detachments from the:
Sixth Regiment (Captain McChesney)
Fourteenth Regiment (Lieutenant Colonel
    Boerstler)
Twentieth Regiment (Major Taylor, Second in
    Command), 1 officer
Twenty-Third Regiment (Captain Roach)
New York Militia Regiments (Major Chapin)
Second Light Dragoons (Cornet Byrd)
Light Artillery (Captain McDowell), 1 x 12-pounder,
    1x 6-pounder
Supply Wagons (2)

The preserved home of the Secord Family in Queenston. This was the starting point of Laura Secord's famous trek to warn Fitzgibbon — now a museum (not a candy shop!).

(Fourteenth Infantry Regiment). His orders were to march some eighteen miles (27 kilometers) behind the British right flank to Beaver Dams. There his troops were to seize the DeCew house that was being used as a forward headquarters and supply depot, and, if possible, eliminate FitzGibbon's and any other Allied forces found in that vicinity. Led by a party of irregular troops from the Buffalo area under Major Cyrenius Chapin, Boerstler and his force of almost 700 men[1] left Fort George late in the day on June 23, 1813, under a pall of heavy rain, which slowed their advance to a mud-caked crawl. Stopping for the night at Queenston, the troops occupied most of the village's buildings and attempted to dry themselves off in preparation for the following day's march to Beaver Dams.

Despite earlier extensive preparations to ensure the secrecy of this mission, lax security at this crucial time allowed a Canadian militia officer, James Secord, and his wife Laura (upon whose unwilling hospitality the American commanders had billeted themselves) to get details of the planned attack. Because James had been invalided by a wound suffered at the battle of Queenston Heights the previous October, it was left to Mrs. Secord to take on the dangerous and arduous duty of passing through the American cordon of sentries undetected and then cross the intervening fifteen miles (24 kilometers) of dense bush and swampland to find and warn FitzGibbon of the impending threat. Subsequent accounts of this trek are contradictory to say the least, but extrapolating from some of the more reliable sources, she began her journey (without the apocryphal dairy cow, daughter, or niece) by walking to her brother's house in St. Davids. She then detoured around any American patrols on the direct road to Beaver Dams by taking the road to Shipman's Corners (St. Catharines). This led her through the southern fringe of the quagmire of the Black Swamp where she was forced to hide in the underbrush and foetid water to avoid detection. From Shipman's, Laura Secord abandoned the roads altogether, cutting across country and following the meandering line of the Twelve Mile Creek

The memorial column at Laura Secord's grave, located within the Drummond Hill Cemetery at Lundy's Lane, Niagara Falls.

through several miles of dense bush, until she eventually reached the foot of the overgrown rock face of the escarpment. Undaunted, Laura Secord scaled the broken and dangerous heights and eventually, completely exhausted, came across a party of Native warriors and was brought to FitzGibbon.

BRITISH / NATIVE ALLIES FORCE, BATTLE OF BEAVER DAMS, JUNE 24, 1813[*2]

British Regulars
49th Regiment (Lieutenant FitzGibbon), 1 officer, 46 other ranks

Canadian Militia
Estimate of 6–10 other ranks

Native Allies (Dominique Ducharme, John Brant)
Six Nations bands, 203 warriors
River Thames bands, 12 warriors
Rice Lake bands, 70 warriors
Lower Canada bands, 180 warriors
In contrast, Norton's account of Native participation in this action refers to:

> ... two hundred and Eighty men from the Villages of Caghnawague, — Kaneghsatague & St. Reges, — about one hundred from the Grand River, and about sixty Chippawas & Messisagas. There were five killed and many wounded.

Alerted to the approaching danger, FitzGibbon had only a handful of regular troops at his command and could easily have abandoned his position in the face of overwhelming odds. Instead he coordinated with the combined force of Upper and Lower Canada Native warriors to ambush the Americans and make the main attack, while he and his few men, accompanied by a handful of militia volunteers, provided fire support.[*2] At the same time, messengers were sent post-haste to Twelve Mile Creek, requesting Major De Haren bring up additional troops to counter the American movement.

After marching a mile past the village of St. Davids, the American column ascended the escarpment and continued toward Beaver Dams, following a rough trackway, unaware that they were under enemy observation. Inevitably, the column became strung out on the march, with Chapin's mounted infantry ending up several hundred yards ahead of the main body. Allowing the entire column to pass by, the hidden Natives sprang their ambush in a heavily wooded section of the trail, where it was impossible for the American units to deploy, or their cavalry to manoeuvre. After making an unsuccessful attempt to retire and drive off those Natives cutting off their retreat, the Americans were forced to continue forward until they finally reached a small clearing, having suffered a number of casualties along the way. Thoroughly discomposed by the Native's continual bloodthirsty screeches and firing, the American infantry formed two ragged lines, back to back. But without any target to fire at, they could only fire blindly toward the woods, while their own numbers continued to diminish as the hidden enemy now had a bigger target to aim at. During the next three hours, the American artillery pieces fired away almost all of their ammunition into the woods, while several attempts were made by the infantry to advance with the bayonet. However, as the warriors simply faded into the woods and then reappeared elsewhere around the encircling noose, these measures had no result other than to break up the American formation into smaller units that were eventually left without ammunition and more vulnerable to the sniping fire that was slowly picking them off. Nor, according to some sources, were Chapin's mounted militia of much use, as they were later accused of hiding amongst the supply wagons instead of supporting the infantry — an accusation Chapin vehemently denied, claiming instead that his force repeatedly drove off parties of the enemy before being ordered back to the wagons by Boerstler.[3]

At this critical juncture, Lieutenant FitzGibbon and his small body of troops also opened fire on the disorganized Americans. In short order, the Americans found themselves surrounded by an unknown number of enemy forces and under the distinct threat of falling beneath the knives of the Native warriors. Little wonder then that when FitzGibbon stepped out around noon, claiming to speak for Major De Haren and demanding the immediate surrender of the American force, Boerstler and his men took it very seriously. Unwilling to see his men turned over to the Native warriors, Boerstler, despite being twice wounded during the engagement and requiring medical attention, still took the time to demand assurances they would come under the protection of the British troops after laying down their arms.

FitzGibbon was nervous about this bluff, as he could not hope to gain any surrender if the paucity of his numbers were revealed, and when Boerstler demanded to see the major, or at least the size of FitzGibbon's force, before surrendering, he was placed in an awkward position. Fortunately, an advance rider from Major De Haren had just arrived and this young officer, Lieutenant John Le Couteur (104th Regiment), fell in with the ruse, claiming that 700 men of the Light Division were immediately at hand. Still not convinced, Boerstler maintained his demand to formally surrender to a visible foe. By using additional delaying tactics, FitzGibbon was able to stall Boerstler for a further hour until De Haren actually arrived and a formal surrender was concluded.[*4]

Unwilling to become prisoners, a number of Chapin's detachment, accompanied by men from the American cavalry, finally took the initiative and galloped from the field, leaving the infantrymen to their fate.[5]

Despite the fact that Beaver Dams was effectively a Native victory, British official reviews of the action failed to properly credit the Natives for their magnificent efforts, nor were the Native allies impressed by the British ban on acquiring trophies of property from their prisoners following the action. As a result, many disgruntled warriors quit the frontier and returned to their homes, thus reducing the number of fighting troops available for combat, while still maintaining the numbers of Natives relying on British food supplies for their sustenance.

ESTIMATED CASUALTIES,
BATTLE OF BEAVER DAMS, JUNE 24, 1813[*4]

British Regulars and Canadian Militias
None

Native Allies

Killed:	est. 15–20 warriors
Wounded:	est. 25–40 warriors

American

Killed:	30 all ranks
Wounded:	est. 70 all ranks
Prisoners:	23 officers, 2 drummers, 487 other ranks
Militia Prisoners Paroled:	30 other ranks

CHAPTER 9

Tightening the Noose:
The Beginning of the Siege of Fort George

Although General Dearborn's health had improved sufficiently to allow him to resume his command duties by early July, the debacle at Beaver Dams proved to be the last straw for his superiors in Washington. In a terse and offensive note, they dismissed the general from his command. At a farewell ceremony, attended by most of his supporting subordinates, Dearborn took an emotional leave of his army and recrossed the Niagara River. To replace Dearborn, Major General James Wilkinson, another Revolutionary War veteran, was appointed. However, Wilkinson was not only highly reluctant to take up this new post, but was stationed in the far south of the country. After being forced to accept his new duty by Secretary of War Armstrong, he deliberately procrastinated in making the appropriate arrangements to take up his new post and then turned his journey north into a leisurely meander, with lengthy stops at numerous places along the way to socialize with prominent politicians and friends. In fact, he did not arrive at Sackets Harbor until August 28th of that year. As a result, until Wilkinson could arrive, command responsibility continued to fall upon Brigadier General John Boyd. Although Boyd was a competent soldier with over 5,500 effective troops, he found himself shackled by Armstrong, who expressly forbade Boyd from engaging in any action with the enemy that could be avoided, and ordered him to maintain an entirely defensive posture against the growing incursions of a numerically inferior but increasingly bold enemy. This course of action greatly dispirited Boyd's troops and led

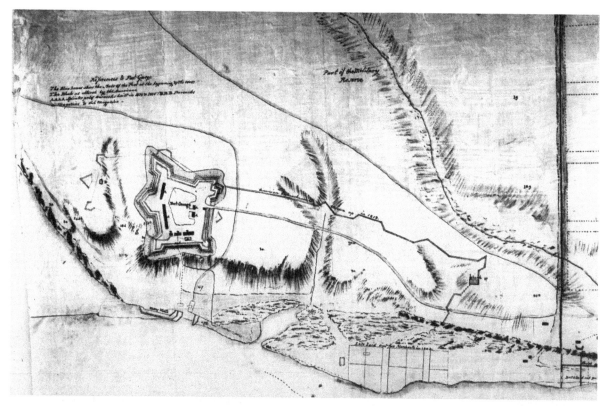

A detail from an 1816 map, showing the alterations made to Fort George (left) following its capture by the Americans in May 1813 and the remains of the adjacent American siege lines erected during the course of that summer as part of the siege of Fort George (centre). The village of Newark (Niagara-on-the-Lake) lies off map to the right (north) and the Niagara River flows across the bottom from left (south) to right (north).

to a crisis of confidence that was clearly recorded in their letters and accounts.

> Every night our troops have a skirmish with the British regulars. They are very troublesome. They keep our troop under arms which exhausts them very much…. Our men are in a wretched condition for clothing. Many barefoot and half-naked. The supplies of the army from

the quartermaster-general's department are irregular…. The weather is very wet. It rains at least one-half the time. The atmosphere is very changeable from very warm to cool days and nights. This produces sickness in the troops.[1]

—Unknown American Officer, June 29, 1813

… the enemy has advanced within a few miles of us. The Indians are continually attacking our picket guard. They are far too strong for us to attack them in the woods.[2]

— Unknown American Officer, July 11, 1813

… the army are panic-stricken and the affairs of this frontier most critical.[3]

— General Peter B. Porter to Governor Tompkins, July 17, 1813

On the other hand, within the British camp the singular turn of events of the past few weeks led to an entire reversal of the previous defeatist attitudes that were so prevalent only a month before. In an immediate attempt to restore confidence and prepare his troops for action, Major General Baron Francis De Rottenburg ordered detachments of the Glengarry Light Infantry, Royal Artillery, and the 19th Light Dragoons to be moved up from Kingston to York, where the entire military garrison had, since the fall of the town in April, consisted principally of the men of Captain Jarvie's company of Incorporated Militia. De Rottenburg also issued additional directives that clearly indicated his determination to take the war in Upper Canada to a whole new level, as well as indulge his personal enthusiasm and expertise for using formations of highly trained skirmishers or "Light" troops, as opposed to the more rigid formations of "Line" battalions.

General Orders, Kingston, 15 June, 1813 …

The Light Company of the 100th Regiment is to proceed to Kingston to join the Light Battalion and the Light Company of the 89th Regiment is to form part of the second Light Battalion. All of the 104th Regiment fit for field service are to be sent forward by detachment as they arrive at Quebec, to join their regiment. The company of the Royal Sappers and Miners is directed to proceed to Kingston….[4]

General Orders, Kingston, 17 June 1813 ...

All officers arriving from Europe and
all recruits and soldiers fit for service
belonging to regiments in Upper Canada
are ordered to proceed to join their
Corps with the least possible delay....[5]

The results of which are best summated in a
letter written by Lieutenant MacEwen (1st [Royal
Scots] Regiment) to his wife in Montreal.

Carrying Place, 23 June 1813 ...

I arrived here this morning in good health
after a march of nearly one hundred
miles from Kingston. Our destination I
cannot at present give you the smallest
information of, as the whole army is on
the march against the enemy, who are at
Fort George....[6]

In part three of this series, *The Flames of War*,
the results of this British offensive and the continued seesawing of military advantage for control
of Upper Canada during the remainder of the year
will be continued.

NOTES

A star indicates the note refers to a sidebar.

ABBREVIATIONS:

LAC: Library and Archives of Canada.

AOO: Archives of Ontario.

CRDH: Ernest Cruikshank, *The Documentary History of the Campaigns upon the Niagara Frontier 1812–1814*, 9 Volumes (Welland, ON: Tribune Press, 1896–1908).

CGMC: Buffalo and Erie County Historical Society Archives, B00-11, A. Conger Goodyear War of 1812 Manuscripts, 1779–1862.

SBD1812: William C.H. Wood, *Select British Documents of the War of 1812* (Toronto: Champlain Society of Canada, 1920).

CHAPTER 2: PRE-EMPTIVE STRIKES

1.   George Prentice, *Henry Clay* (Hartford, CT: Samuel Hammer Jr., 1831), 98–99.

2.   Alexander C. Casselman, ed., *Richardson's War of 1812*, Vol. 1 (Toronto: Historical Publishing Co., 1902), facsimile edition by Coles Publishing Co., Toronto, 1974, 132; Sandy Antal, *A Wampum Denied, Proctor's War of 1812* (Ottawa: Carleton University Press, 1997), 164.

3.   *Ibid.*

4.   A. Hough, *History of St. Lawrence and Franklin Counties, New York, 1760–1814* (Albany, NY: Little & Co., 1853), 625–26.

*5. *Ibid.*; CRDH, Vol. 5, 74–77.

*6. *Ibid.*

7.   CRDH, Vol. 5, 80.

8.   *Ibid.*

CHAPTER 3: SETTING THE PENDULUM IN MOTION

1.   J. Brannan, *Official Letters of the Military and Naval Officers of the United States, During the War with Great*

Britain in the Years 1812, 13, 14, & 15 (Washington, DC: Way & Gideon, 1823), 133–34.

*2. Carl Benn, *Historic Fort York, 1793–1993* (Toronto: Natural Heritage/Natural History Inc., 1993), 50; B. Lossing, *Pictorial Field Book of the War of 1812* (New York: Harper and Brothers, 1868), 27.

*3. Carl Benn, *Historic Fort York, 1793–1993* (Toronto: Natural Heritage/Natural History Inc., 1993); LAC, RG8-I: British Military and Naval Records, 1757–1903, Vol. 695, 202.

*4. J. Brannan, *Official Letters of the Military and Naval Officers of the United States, during the War with Great Britain in the years 1812, 13, 14, & 15* (Washington, DC: Way & Gideon, 1823), 144–45; CRDH, Vol. 5, 162.

*5. CRDH, Vol. 5, 165–66, 183, 215; LAC, RG8-I: British Military and Naval Records, 1757–1903, Vol. 695, 57, 166, 192; and J.L. Thomson, *Historical Sketches of the Late War Between the United States and Great Britain* (Philadelphia: Thomas Delsilver, 1816), 127–28.

CHAPTER 4: LINE VERSUS LINE, THE BATTLE OF FORT GEORGE MAY 27, 1813

*1. CRDH, Vol. 5, 221.

2. *Ibid.*, 218 (Lt. Col. Bruyeres, Royal Engineers, to Sir G. Prevost, February 13, 1813).

*3. J.P. Boyd, *Documents and Facts Relative to Military Events during the Late War* (Private Publishing, 1816), 3, 13; CRDH, Vol. 6, 28–30.

*4. CRDH, Vol. 5, 257–58; Colonel G.W.L. Nicholson, *The Fighting Newfoundlander* (Government of Newfoundland, 1963), 73–77.

*5. CRDH, Vol. 5, 247–48, 253; Government of the United States, *Causes of the Failure of the Army on the Northern Frontier*, Report to the House of Representatives February 2, 1814, 13th Congress, 2nd Session, Military Affairs, 444–45; J.P. Boyd, *Documents and Facts Relative to Military Events during the Late War* (Private Publishing, 1816), 5; J. Brannan, *Official Letters of the Military and Naval Officers of the United States, during the War with*

Great Britain in the years 1812, 13, 14, & 15 (Washington, DC: Way & Gideon, 1823), 162; and W. James, *A Full and Correct Account of the Military Occurrences of the Late War between Great Britain and the United States of America*, Vol. 3 (London: William James, 1818), 159, 410.

6. J. Armstrong, *Notices of the War of 1812* (New York: Wiley & Putnam, 1840), 134.

7. *Ibid.*

8. CGMC, Vol. 11, Usher Parsons, "Diary of Naval Surgeon," Entry for May 28, 1813.

CHAPTER 5: VICTORIES, BUT FOR WHOM?

1. Sandy Antal, *A Wampum Denied, Proctor's War of 1812* (Ottawa: Carleton University Press, 1997), 222.

2. C. Elliott, *Winfield Scott, the Soldier and the Man* (Toronto, The Macmillan Company of Canada Ltd., 1937), 40.

3. LAC, RG8-I: British Military and Naval Records, 1757–1903, Vol. 695, 43.

*4. Patrick Wilder, *The Battle of Sackett's Harbour* (Baltimore: The Nautical & Aviation Publishing Company of America, 1994), 71–75.

*5. *Ibid.*, 80–81; CRDH, Vol. 5, 283.

6. CRDH, Vol. 5, 285–86.

7. *Ibid.*

*8. CRDH, Vol. 5, 278; Patrick Wilder, *The Battle of Sackett's Harbour* (Baltimore: The Nautical & Aviation Publishing Company of America, 1994), 71–75.

9. CRDH, Vol. 5, 292–94.

10. CRDH, Vol. 6, 4–5.

11. CRDH, Vol. 6, 139.

12. *Ibid.*

CHAPTER 6: CONFUSION IN THE DARKNESS, THE BATTLE OF STONEY CREEK, JUNE 6, 1813

1. John Kearsley, *Memoir of Major John Kearsley*, Clement Library, University of Michigan, 3–4.

*2. *Niles Register*, Vol. 11, 116–19; CRDH, Vol. 6, 8–11; Government of the United States, *Causes of the Failure of the Army on the Northern Frontier*, Report to the House of Representatives February 2, 1814, 13th Congress, 2nd Session, Military Affairs, 447; and James Elliott, *Strange Fatality: The Battle of Stoney Creek, 1813* (Toronto, Robin Brass Studio Inc., 2009), 259–63.

3. CRDH, Vol. 6, 50–51 (Letter from an unidentified officer to the editor, *United States Gazette*), July 8, 1813.

4. CRDH, Vol. 6, 13 (Lieutenant J. Fitzgibbon to Rev. J. Somerville, Montreal, June 7, 1813).

5. John Kearsley, *Memoir of Major John Kearsley*, Clement Library, University of Michigan, 6–8.

6. SBD1812, Vol. 3, Part 2, 524.

7. CRDC, Vol. 6, 13 (Lieutenant J. Fitzgibbon to Rev. J. Somerville, Montreal, June 7, 1813).

8. Government of the United States, *Causes of the Failure of the Army on the Northern Frontier*, Report to the House of Representatives February 2, 1814, 13th Congress, 2nd Session, Military Affairs, 447 (Colonel James Burn to Major General Dearborn [extract, letter No. 2] American State Papers, Military Affairs).

CHAPTER 7: THE PENDULUM SWINGS BACK

1. Ernest Cruikshank, *The Blockade of Fort George, 1813*, Niagara Historical Society Papers, No. 3, 1898, 40.

2. Government of the United States, *Causes of the Failure of the Army on the Northern Frontier*, Report to the House of Representatives February 2, 1814, 13th Congress, 2nd Session, Military Affairs, 455–58.

3. *Ibid.*
4. *Ibid.*
5. *Ibid.*
6. *Ibid.*
7. *Ibid.*
8. *Ibid.*
9. *Ibid.*
10. CRDH, Vol. 6, 63.

*11. Government of the United States, *Causes of the Failure of the Army on the Northern Frontier*, Report to the House of Representatives February 2, 1814, 13th Congress, 2nd Session, Military Affairs, 447; CRDH, Vol. 6, 11, 25; and W. James, *A Full and Correct Account of the Military Occurrences of the Late War between Great Britain and the United States of America*, Vol. 3 (London: William James, 1818), 410.

CHAPTER 8: THE WARNING MUST BE GIVEN, THE BATTLE OF BEAVER DAMS, JUNE 24, 1813

*1. LAC, RG8-I: British Military and Naval Records, 1757–1903, Vol. 679, 137; W. James, *A Full and Correct Account of the Military Occurrences of the Late War between Great Britain and the United States of America*, Vol. 3 (London: William James, 1818), 159, 438–39.

*2. *Ibid.*; Carl F. Klinck, *Journal of Major John Norton*, Publication No. 46 (Toronto: Champlain Society of Canada, 1970), 332.

3. C. Chapin, *Chapin's Review of Armstrong's Notices of the War of 1812* (Black Rock, NY: Private Publication, 1836), 12–13; Carl F. Klinck, *Journal of Major John Norton*, Publication No. 46 (Toronto: Champlain Society of Canada, 1970), 332.

*4. LAC, RG8-I: British Military and Naval Records, 1757–1903, Vol. 1219, 76 and Vol. 679, 137.

5. C. Chapin, *Chapin's Review of Armstrong's Notices of the War of 1812* (Black Rock, NY: Private Publication, 1836), 12–13.

CHAPTER 9: TIGHTENING THE NOOSE

1. Ernest Cruikshank, *The Blockade of Fort George, 1813* (Niagara Historical Society Papers, No. 3, 1898), 42–44.

2. *Ibid.*
3. *Ibid.*
4. CRDH, Vol. 6, 87.
5. *Ibid.*, 90.
6. *Ibid.*, 97.

SELECTED BIBLIOGRAPHY

PRIMARY SOURCES

Archival
1. Library and Archives of Canada
   Manuscript Groups (MG)
   MG10A: U.S. Department of State, War of 1812
   Records
   MG11 (CO42): British Colonial Office, Original
   Correspondence, Canada
   MG11 (CO47): Upper Canada Records, 1764–1836,
   Miscellaneous
   MG13 (WO62): Commissariat Dept, Miscellaneous
   Records 1809–1814
   MG19/A39: Duncan Clark Papers
   MG24/A9: Sir George Prevost Papers

   Research Groups (RG)
   RG5-A1: Civil Secretary's Office, Upper Canada
   Sundries, 1791–1867
   RG8-I: British Military and Naval Records, 1757–
   1903
   RG9-I: Pre-Confederation Records, Military

RG10: Indian Department Records
RG19/E5A: Department of Finance, War of 1812,
Losses Board

2. Archives Ontario
   MS35/1: Strachan Papers
   MS74/R5: Merritt Papers
   MS501: Thorburn Papers
   MS58: Band Papers
   MS500: Street Papers
   MS519: Joel Stone Papers
   MS520: Solomon Jones Papers
   MS502/B Series: Nelles Papers
   MU2099: A.A. Rapelje Papers
   MU527: Duncan Clark Papers
   MU2034: Events in the Military History of the Saint
   Lawrence River Valley 1779–1814.
   MS74.R5: Henry Ruttan Papers
   Microfilm B91/Reel 1: Table of Statutes, Upper
   Canada Legislature 1792–1840

3. Metro Toronto Reference Library
   Hagerman, C.: Journal of Christopher Hagerman

MacDonell, G.: MacDonell Papers
Prevost Papers, 7 Vols., S108, Cub 7

4. Detroit Public Library Archives
Kirby, J.: James Kirby Papers

5. Buffalo and Erie County Historical Society Archives, A.
Conger Goodyear War of 1812 Manuscripts, 1779–1862,
Mss. BOO-11. 16 Volumes

EARLY SECONDARY PUBLICATIONS

Armstrong, J. *Notices of the War of 1812.* New York: Wiley & Putnam, 1840.

Blakeslee, S. "Narrative of Colonel Samuel Blakeslee; A Defender of Buffalo in the War of 1812." In *Publications of the Buffalo Historical Society, Volume 8.* Buffalo, NY: Bigelow Brothers, 1905.

Boyd, J.P. *Documents and Facts Relative to Military Events During the Late War.* Privately published, 1816.

Brackenridge, Henry. M. *History of the Late War Between the United States and Great Britain.* Cushing & Jewett, 1817.

Brannan, J. *Official Letters of the Military and Naval Officers of the United States, during the War with Great Britain in the years 1812, 13, 14, & 15.* Washington D.C.: Way & Gideon, 1823.

Chapin, C. *Chapin's Review of Armstrong's Notices of the War of 1812.* Black Rock, NY: B.F. Adams, 1836.

Davis, Paris M. *An Authentick History of the Late War Between the United States and Great Britain.* Ithica, NY: Mack & Andrus, 1829.

_____. *The Four Principal Battles of the Late War Between the United States and Great Britain.* Harrisburg, NY: Jacob Baab, 1832.

Dawson, M. *A Historical Narrative of the True Civil and Military Services of Major-General William H. Harrison.* Cincinnati: *Cincinnati Advertiser* Office, 1824.

Dearborn H.A.S. *Defence of Gen. Henry Dearborn: against the attack of Gen. William Hull.* Boston: E.W. Davies, 1824.

Hitsman, J.M. *History of the American War of Eighteen Hundred and Twelve.* Philadelphia, PA: W. McCarty, 1816.

James, W. *A Full and Correct Account of the Military Occurrences of the Late War Between Great Britain and the United States of America.* London: William James, 1818.

Johnson, Frederick H. *A Guide for Every Visitor to Niagara Falls.* Niagara Falls: Self-published, 1852.

Lossing, Benson. *Pictorial Field Book of the War of 1812.* New York: Harper and Brothers, 1868.

McCarty, W. *History of the American War of 1812.* Philadelphia, PA: William McCarty & Davis, 1817.

Merritt, William Hamilton. *Journal of Events: Principally on the Detroit & Niagara Frontiers During the War of 1812.* St. Catharines, CW: Canada West Historical Society, 1863.

Morgan, J.C. *The Emigrant's Guide, With Recollections of Upper and Lower Canada During the Late War Between the United States of America and Great Britain.* London: Longman, Hurst, Rees, Orme & Brown, 1824.

O'Connor, T. *An Impartial and Correct History of the War Between the United States of America and Great Britain.* Belfast: Joseph Smyth, 1816. Reprint of the John Low edition, New York, 1815.

Perkins, S. *A History of the Political and Military Events of the Late War Between the United States and Great Britain.* New Haven, CT: S. Converse, 1825.

"Proceedings and Debates of the House of Representatives of the United States." 12th Congress, 1st Session (1812). U.S. Government Records.

Ripley, E.A. *Facts Relative to the Campaign on the Niagara in 1814.* Boston: Self-published, 1815.

Scott, Winfield. *Memoirs of Lieut. General Scott.* Sheldon & Co., 1864.

Sturtevant, I. *Barbarities of the Enemy Exposed in a report of the Committee of the House of Representatives of the United States.* Worcester, MA: Remark Dunnell, 1814.

Thomson, J.L. *Historical Sketches of the Late War between the United States and Great Britain.* Philadelphia, PA: Thomas Delsilver, 1816.

Wilkinson, J. *Diagrams and Plans Illustrative of the Principal Battles of the War of 1812.* Philadelphia: Self-published, 1815.

SECONDARY SOURCES

Later Secondary Publications

Buell, W. "Military Movements in Eastern Ontario During the War of 1812." *Ontario Historical Society, Papers and Records*, Vol. 10 (1913) and Vol. 17 (1919).

Carnochan, Janet. "Reminiscences of Niagara and St. Davids." Niagara Historical Society, Paper No. 20 (1911).

Crooks, James. "Recollections of the Late Hon. James Crooks." Niagara Historical Society Papers, No. 28, c.1916.

Cruickshank, Ernest. "A Memoir of Colonel the Honourable James Kerby, His Life in Letters." Welland County Historical Society, *Papers and Records*, No. 4, 1931.

————. "The Battle of Fort George." Niagara Historical Society, Paper No. 12, 1912. Reprint by Niagara Historical Society, 1990.

————. "The Blockade of Fort George." Niagara Historical Society, Paper No. 3.

————. "Campaigns of 1812–1814." Niagara Historical Society, Paper No. 9, 1902.

————. "Letters of 1812 from the Dominion Archives." Niagara Historical Society, Paper No. 23, 1913.

Dorsheimer, W. "The Village of Buffalo during the War of 1812." Presentation to the Buffalo Historical Society, 1863.

"Family History and Reminiscences of Early Settlers and Recollections of the War of 1812." Niagara Historical Society, Paper No. 28, 1915.

Government of the United States. "Causes of the Failure of the Army on the Northern Frontier." Report to the House of Representatives, February 2, 1814, 13th Congress, 2nd Session, Military Affairs.

"Historic Houses." Niagara Historical Society, Paper No. 5, 1899.

"Jarvis Papers." Women's Canadian Historical Society of Toronto Papers and Transactions, Transaction No. 5 (1902), 3–9.

Kilborn, John. "Accounts of the War of 1812." In Thaddeus W.H. Leavitt. *History of Leeds and Grenville Counties from 1749 to 1879.* Brockville, ON: Recorder Press, 1879.

"Reminiscences of Arthur Galloway." Cornell University Library, Ithaca, NY. New York State Historical Monographs, Historical Literature Collection, Anonymous collection, *circa* 1850.

"Reminiscences of Niagara." Niagara Historical Society, Paper No. 11, 1904.

Severence, F.H., ed. "Papers Relating to the War of 1812 on the Niagara Frontier." Buffalo Historical Society Publications, Vol. 5, 1902.

Severence, F.H., ed. "The Case of Brigadier General Alexander Smyth." Buffalo Historical Society Publications, Vol. 18, 1941.

Warner, Robert I. "Memoirs of Capt. John Lampman and His Wife Mary Secord." Welland County Historical Society, *Papers and Records, Vol. 3* (1927), 126–34.

Wright, Ross Pier, *"The Burning of Dover."* Unpublished manuscript, 1948.

Books

Adams, Henry. *History of the United States of America During the Administrations of Madison.* New York: Library of America, 1986. Reprint of original 1891 volumes.

Antal, Sandy. *A Wampum Denied, Proctor's War of 1812.* Ottawa: Carleton University Press, 1997.

Auchinleck, George. *A History of the War Between Great Britain and the United States of America During the Years 1812, 1813 & 1814.* Toronto: Thomas Maclear, 1853. Reprint by Arms & Armour Press and Pendragon House, 1972.

Babcock, Louis L. *The War of 1812 on the Niagara Frontier, Volume 29.* Buffalo, NY: Buffalo Historical Society Publications, 1927.

Benn, Carl. *The Iroquois in the War of 1812.* Toronto: University of Toronto Press, 1998.

Bingham, Robert. W. *The Cradle of the Queen City: A History of*

Buffalo to the Incorporation of the City, Volume 31. Buffalo, NY: Buffalo Historical Society Publications, 1931.

Bowler, R. Arthur, ed. *Essays on the War of 1812 and Its Legacy.* Youngstown, NY: Old Fort Niagara Association, 1991.

Brant, Irving. *The Fourth President: A Life of James Madison.* Indianapolis & New York: The Bobbs Merrill Company, 1970.

Casselman, Alexander C., ed. *Richardson's War of 1812.* Toronto: Historical Publishing Co., 1902. Facsimile edition by Coles Publishing Co., Toronto, 1974.

"Contest for the Command of Lake Ontario in 1812 & 1813." Transactions of the Royal Society of Canada, SEC II, Series III, Vol. X.

Cruikshank, Ernest. *The Documentary History of the Campaigns upon the Niagara Frontier in 1812–1814.* Welland, ON: Tribune Press, 1896–1908. Nine volumes.

Elliott, C. *Winfield Scott, the Soldier and the Man.* Toronto: The Macmillan Company of Canada Ltd., 1937.

Gayler, Hugh J., ed. *Niagara's Changing Landscapes.* Ottawa: Carleton University Press, 1994.

Gilleland, J.C. *History of the Late War Between the United States and Great Britain.* Baltimore, MD: Schaeffer & Maund, 1817.

Gourlay, Robert. *Statistical Account of Upper Canada Compiled with a View to a Grand System of Emigration.* London: Simpkin and Marshall, 1822. Two Volumes. Republished by the Social Science Research Council of Canada, S.R. Publishers Ltd., Johnson Reprint Corp. 1966.

Graves, D.E. *Fix Bayonets! A Royal Welch Fusilier at War 1796–1815.* Montreal: Robin Brass Studio, 2006.

Hitsman, J. Mackay. *The Incredible War of 1812: A Military History.* Toronto: Robin Brass Studio, 1999. Revised edition, updated by Donald Graves.

Horsman, R. *The Causes of the War of 1812.* New York: A.S. Barnes and Co., 1962.

Hough, Franklin B. *A History of St. Lawrence and Franklin Counties, New York.* Albany, NY: Little & Co., 1853.

Illustrated Historical Atlas of Norfolk County. Toronto: H. Belden & Co., 1877.

Illustrated Historical Atlas of the Counties of Frontenac, Lennox and Addington. Toronto: J.H. Meachan & Co., 1878.

Illustrated Historical Atlas of the Counties of Hastings & Prince Edward. Toronto: H. Belden & Co., 1878.

Illustrated Historical Atlas of the Counties of Lincoln and Welland. Toronto: H.R. Page, 1876.

Illustrated Historical Atlas of the Counties of Northumberland and Durham. Toronto: H. Belden & Co., 1877.

Illustrated Historical Atlas of the Counties of Stormont, Dundas & Glengarry. Toronto: Belden & Co. Toronto, 1879.

Irving, L.H. *Officers of the British Forces in Canada during the War of 1812.* Toronto: Canadian Military Institute, 1908.

Klinck, Carl F. *Journal of Major John Norton.* Toronto: Champlain Society of Canada, 1970. Publication No. 46.

Leavitt. T.W.H. *History of Leeds and Grenville Counties from 1749 to 1879.* Brockville, ON: Recorder Press, 1879.

Mackay, J. *The Incredible War of 1812.* Toronto: University of Toronto, 1965.

Malcomson, Robert. *A Very Brilliant Affair: The Battle of Queenston Heights, 1812.* Toronto, Robin Brass Studio, 2003.

_____. *Lords of the Lake: The Naval War on Lake Ontario, 1812–1814.* Toronto: Robin Brass Studio, 1998.

Ridout Edgar, Lady Matilda, Thomas Ridout. *Ten Years in Upper Canada in Peace & War, 1805–1815. Being the Ridout Letters with Annotations by Matilda Edgar.* Toronto: William Brigs, 1890.

Ruttan, Henry. *Reminiscences of the Hon. Henry Ruttan: Loyalist Narratives from Upper Canada.* Toronto: Champlain Society, 1946.

Stagg, J.C.A. *Mr. Madison's War: Politics, Diplomacy, and Warfare in the Early American Republic 1783–1830.* Princeton, NJ: Princeton University Press, 1983.

Stanley, George F.G. *The War of 1812: Land Operations.* Toronto: Macmillan of Canada and the Canadian War Museum 1983.

Wood, William C.H. *Select British Documents of the War of 1812.* Toronto: Champlain Society of Canada, 1920. Three volumes.

INDEX